THE PRACTICAL GUIDE TO BUYING DIAMONDS

By *Jay Feder*
In Denver
534-0251
1-800-841-7283
1-800-841-SAVE

Call for free information
on prices and quotes.

Designed by Kristie Iverson
Cartoons by Mike Pemberton
Illustrations by Anne Clark

The Four C's Press, Denver, Colorado

ISBN   0-9619478-0-2

Library of Congress   88-111966

The Practical Guide To Buying Diamonds

The Four C's Press/November 1986

Published by The Four C's Press
            910 16th Street/Suite 335
            Denver, CO 80202
                    • Inside Colorado (303) 534-0251
Printed in the United States of America

This book is dedicated to my parents:

To Mollie and Manny Feder, may they rest in peace. My mother was an outstanding woman whose entire being radiated love, warmth, kindness and fire.

My father was a wonderful man who was the embodiment of strength, courage, gentleness and faith.

Together they were an incredible loving partnership and we will forever miss them dearly.

I pray that I will succeed in offering a fraction of the inspiration and help to my children that my parents have given to me.

Last but not least, I dedicate this book to my second mother, Edith Lustig Feder. She's a woman of beauty, compassion, sensitivity and a heart of gold. May she live a long, healthy life with only joy and happiness. She deserves that and more.

Many, many thanks:

To my life partner, Celia, who deserves most of the credit for whatever I have accomplished. She is a genuine woman of valor at home and in business.

To my loyal crew at Jay Feder Jewelers. Brenda Abel, Douglas and Kathi Geivett, Cami Griffith, Debbie Leo, Natalie Oleksiuk, Jim Peelor, Lil Sonntag Powers, Ray Raub, Debby Robinson, Adrijana Sedivy, John and Jennifer Sholl ... you're the greatest!

And finally, to all my friends and relatives who have helped me in this project. Your encouragement, advice and moral support were priceless.

PREFACE

The common complaint voiced by consumers is that their only source of diamond and jewelry information is their local jewelry merchant, and, in effect, that leaves the fox guarding the chicken coop. I've noticed the trend toward educated consumerism and in my business I've begun to encourage my customers to use their own judgment. In order to do that, they must know how! I have therefore written a simple, practical guide to diamond buying, based on years of explaining this practical material to thousands of my own customers.

This includes (1) detailed information on the 4 Cs of the grading of diamonds, (2) how to know the real value of a diamond and how to determine what type of stone is best suited for your purpose, (3) how not to be intimidated by the supposed experts, (4) where to find direct sources to buy diamonds, (5) common myths and misconceptions such as investment schemes, etc. All this material is offered with a liberal dose of my personal experiences gleaned from the kind of painful errors you will be able to avoid after reading this book.

TABLE OF CONTENTS

SECTION 1
*Diamonds Shine Brighter
When You Buy Them for Less!*

SECTION 2
History of Diamonds and Their Investment Value

SECTION 3
*Gold Settings and Colored Stones:
There Are More Facets to Jewelry
Than The Ones On a Diamond*

SECTION I

Diamonds Shine Brighter
When You Buy Them for Less!

INTRODUCTION

Why A Practical Guide
To Diamond And Jewelry Buying?

Would you pay $800 to $1200 for an ounce of pure gold in today's market? Of course not. It depends on what gold is going for on the day you read this book. Spot gold at the time this book went to press was $420 an ounce. You can follow the ups and downs of the gold market by turning on any morning news station. Yet, paying 100 percent or more than market value is exactly what people are doing every single day with a generally much more expensive, natural, refined, world recognized commodity. They do it when they innocently walk into a jewelry store and buy diamonds.

In a consumer oriented society, we don't think twice about questioning the judgment of our doctors, mechanics, stockbrokers, and lawyers. The multitude of do-it-yourself guides in almost every area has made it clear to consumers that they can learn to evaluate independently what the experts are telling them.

This truth applies to a diamond purchase as well. Unquestioning blind trust can result in paying 100, 200, or 300 percent more than a diamond is worth. Learning objective standards of judging diamonds can save you money. It can also give you the gratification of knowing what you're doing in what was formerly an insider's market.

On Shopping

When buying a diamond one should *always* expect to

do some shopping around. It is amazing to see the extreme price differences in the market. Diamonds are not like manufactured items that may vary just slightly. Even in the wholesale market, there may be as much as 40 percent, 50 percent or more in price variation among cutters, second-hand or low wholesale prices. There is yet more variance when you look at high wholesale. This variation is determined by the price the cutters or the wholesalers paid and how much they hope to profit. Only then do the retail mark ups begin.

In most larger cities, it pays to call wholesalers first to see if they will deal directly with the public. Usually you can see more of a selection in unmounted diamonds at much lower prices. (Later I will explain why this is so critical.) The wholesaler doesn't expect the high percentage of return and doesn't have the overhead that warrants it. Consequently, he can offer you a better deal. This does not mean that a retailer can't or won't offer a "good deal" in order to make the sale.

In fact, my experience is that small, privately owned jewelry stores will more likely be willing and able to "deal" than large chain stores. But don't take anything for granted until you've checked it out. When you know what you're looking for, you can spot a "good deal" anywhere.

The purpose of this guide is not to be literary or scientific, but rather to be a useful handbook that will offer practical information and enable consumers to get the most for their money — and have fun doing it.

My hope is that you will learn to view diamonds as a commodity like gold, that, while they have their ups and downs, they do have market value. With the information contained in this book, you can learn to negotiate a price that is fair to your diamond dealer and fair to you.

At the end of this section and at the end of the book you'll find the Diamond Buyer's Checklist which will summarize what you have learned in each chapter. It is organized in the form of questions to ask yourself as you shop. We recommend that you take it along on your shopping trips.

CHAPTER 1

Love Is Blind
But You Don't Have To Be!

If you are like most people, your first diamond purchase is (or was) probably an engagement diamond — one of the most meaningful, emotional and expensive purchases you will have made. Hopefully, it will be cherished for life and may even become an heirloom. You also hope that it will be an item that will appreciate in value as time goes on. In other words, you hope that it will be money well spent; if not an investment, at least a hedge against inflation.

When buying a diamond, most people go to a retail diamond store, staffed by trained sales personnel whose main goal is getting customers to buy an overpriced product. Their selling style discourages comparison shopping. The retail diamond business has long been based on low volume and high mark ups of anywhere from 100 percent to 400 percent. These mark ups, of course, destroy the possibility of buying diamonds as an investment.

In addition, the industry has tried to convince the consumer that only the experts can evaluate diamonds and you must blindly trust your salesperson. Trust, of course, is fundamental. But trust doesn't mean that you should make a blind, uneducated purchase.

Recently, one of the largest diamond store chains ran a Christmas advertising campaign depicting professionals such as a young stereo expert which indicated that while he understands the intricacies of stereos, he can't possibly understand the quality of a diamond. The ad clearly implies that this intelligent young man must blindly trust the diamond store experts, who will not lead him astray. Ironically, this particular chain store is known in the industry for having the highest mark up on its diamonds.

Understanding the basics of diamonds is infinitely simpler than understanding stereos, used cars or almost any other major purchase, *if* a person takes a little time and effort to learn how to evaluate and compare. Often, salespeople are not willing to share this "secret" information for fear of losing those outrageously high profits. Some salespeople simply don't have the knowledge. And then there are some, like myself, who feel that we'll do better in the long run with the customer as a knowledgeable partner.

The purpose of this guide is to give you, the customer, the practical basics of diamond grading and comparison. This information will give you the confidence you need to resist the sophisticated intimidation tactics of some diamond merchants. Ultimately, they need you more than you need them.

This guide will teach you the "tricks of the trade" and tell you how to buy diamonds at near wholesale prices. Diamonds are items of beauty, rarity, and intrinsic value. Buying them is an important and emotionally charged decision but it doesn't mean you should not be rational and well-informed. Remember, love may be blind, but when it comes to buying a diamond, you don't have to be.

Diamonds are Generic — The 6 Cs

The first step in avoiding a blind purchase is to remember just what a diamond is. Although many of the "classier" jewelry establishments will want you to believe differently, *diamonds are generic in nature.* There are no such things as "designer" diamonds. Some may be cut better and all are different, but once you learn to recognize what a diamond is, the name or decor of the jewelry

"Love is blind, but you don't have to be!"

store is of little consequence. The value of a diamond is based on its quality, not its cost. This value is objectively determined.

Recent national publicity campaigns have emphasized the importance of the 4 Cs in purchasing diamonds. The 4 Cs are: 1) Carat weight; 2) Cut; 3) Color; and 4) Clarity. The irony is that most jewelry salespeople are not really able to explain these fundamentals to their customer. Armed with this information you can separate the really trustworthy jewelers who want to give a fair deal from those who give our industry a bad name.

I always tell my customers that there are actually two more Cs that are just as important, if not more so. These additional 2 Cs are: 5) Cost or cash and credit and 6) Common sense. Your understanding of the basics of these Cs will help you compute the value of your purchase. The next chapters will explain how to evaluate the Cs in detail.

Value For Your Dollar — The 4 Cs

The 4 Cs system has developed into an objective method of evaluating diamonds.

It is a method of grading and ultimately judging a diamond's worth as compared to other available diamonds. This system is the key to your diamond's value and your key to buying beautiful jewelry at a fair price.

Diamond grading is fairly simple. An understanding of the 4 Cs will give you the information needed to evaluate a diamond. Adding the 2 Cs of cost and common sense will enable you to determine the fairness of any price and whether you should keep shopping.

Keep in mind that there is no such thing as a good or a bad diamond. Often, the diamond merchant will try to "push" certain diamonds he has in stock and tell you what you need. Don't believe it! As you begin to appreciate the different qualities of diamonds, you will decide what is important to you. Some people prefer size and flash to a finer quality. Others want perfection and will sacrifice size to that end. The important thing is to pay a reasonable market price for what you want.

"Buy it, you'll like it!"

Always begin shopping by clearly telling the salespeople that you are shopping and seriously looking for the best deal. Don't be intimidated by salespeople. If they are not cooperative and willing to prove that they can give you the best deal, move on. They need you more than you need them! Never forget that. Thousands of dollars can hinge on learning that lesson. You deserve the best at the best price. Read on and you'll know how to accomplish just that!

Remember — A diamond is just a piece of coal that made good under pressure! *You can do the same!*

CHAPTER 2
Carat Weight: The First C

Many people who are buying diamonds set a price range for what they are looking for. As you shop for a diamond, you may want to wait and see what cut, color and clarity you prefer, and then assess the size you can afford within these parameters.

The first C in diamond grading is carat weight. Carat is a weight, not a size, although a well-cut diamond will appear a certain size and you can usually estimate the weight of the diamond based on its size (see illustration #1). The standard measurement of gemstones is the carat (ct.). A carat weighs 1/5 of a gram. The carat is divided into 100 points. Example: .50 ct. = 50 points = 1/2 ct. This is an international convention which any jeweler will recognize.

4.1 mm
¼ carat

5.15 mm
½ carat

6.5 mm
1 carat

7.4 mm
1 ½ carats

7.8 mm
1 ¼ carats

8.2 mm
2 carats

8.8 mm
2½ carats

9.35 mm
3 carats

Illustration 1

The market has established different milestone values for different weights. Those specific weights, or "magic numbers," are .25 ct., .33 ct., .38 ct., .45 ct., .50 ct., .70 ct., .75 ct., .90 ct., .95 ct., 1.00 ct., 1.50 ct., 2.00 ct., etc. Each time you hit the next "magic number," the price and value per carat will increase significantly. The percentage of change of the price per carat when comparing larger diamonds will vary depending on factors such as supply and demand, availability in the marketplace, and the quality of the stone.

The closer to perfection the diamond gets quality-wise, the more important it is to have a "perfect" size. A perfect .99 ct. diamond is worth only half of the value of a full 1.00 ct. With medium grade stones of the same weight, value will vary 20 to 30 percent. This is a very significant difference and important to remember.

Always try to find out exact weights. A pair of earrings can, according to the industry standard terminology, be advertised as 1/2 ct. when their total weight is as little as .45 ct. or 45 points. A 1 ct. total weight pair may weigh only .95 ct.

The main idea to keep in mind is that a diamond under the "magic number" is worth less than a perfect size. Don't let someone sell you a .97 ct. and tell you it's a "full" one carat or that it has the value of a full 1.00 ct. diamond. A 1.00 ct. should be a full carat, but a "1 ct." can mean a light 1 ct. (a .95 ct. or up). There is nothing wrong with a .97 ct. In fact, it may be perfect for a person who can't afford a full 1.00 ct., but wants the 1.00 ct. look. The price break can be very helpful, **but** — make sure you get that price break.

Also, be aware that a heavy stone like a 1.15 ct. is considered an "off size" in the market because it has extra weight without reaching the next magic number for added value per carat. Both the .97 ct. and the 1.15 ct. may not be the easiest stones for resale. The buyer will negotiate by emphasizing the "off size" status of these diamonds. If you want a little larger stone, or the price break of the smaller one, that's okay as long as you are aware of the key to market value.

Recently, I met a gentleman 3 days after the 30 day guarantee for his new, near perfect .47 ct. certified diamond had expired. Aside from the fact that he paid double the wholesale market price at a so-called "direct import" discount jewelers, no one had explained to him that .47 ct. is a "light" half carat and a very difficult stone for resale. Buying that type of .47 ct. is akin to buying a Rolls Royce without a bumper. At least with the Rolls Royce you can put a bumper back on the car, but there is no way to add the three points to the diamond.

One way to be sure you are getting an exact weight is to ask the salesperson to weigh the loose diamond in front of you. A dealer who specializes in diamonds will most likely welcome your informed questions, and should have a scale readily available.

While this is not the topic of this book, weight is one answer to a common question that people always ask. That is, how do you tell the difference between a real diamond and a CZ — cubic zirconia — the most common and closest diamond imitation? An expert has many different ways to tell the difference, including visual, hardness and an electronic device which measures the thermal conductivity of the stone.

The most definitive way is to weigh the stone. A CZ weighs 70 percent heavier than a diamond. If the stone measures 6.5 mm or the size of a 1 ct. and weighs 1.70 ct. — watch out! You've got a genuine **fake!** Cubic zirconia is proof positive that the most sincere form of flattery is imitation! CZ's have only served to increase people's interest in the real thing!

Back to diamond weights. Diamonds prove that good things come in small packages, but keep in mind that with diamonds, exact carat weight is where it's at. Get the point?

CHAPTER 3

Cut: The Second C

There are actually two important considerations to the cut of a diamond: 1) its shape, and 2) how well it is cut.

Choosing the Cut

A diamond can be cut into almost any shape, such as flowers, butterflies, stars, horse heads, fish, etc. The popular cuts are "round brilliants" and fancy shapes such as marquise shapes, pear shapes, ovals, emerald cuts, radiants, and heart shapes (see illustration #2).

Emerald   Oval   Marquis   Pear   Round

Illustration 2

Set Aside the Setting

As we mentioned earlier, it is much easier to appreciate these shapes when viewing them loose or unmounted. By doing this you will not only be able to assure yourself that the diamond has the value you are paying for, but you will also avoid the distraction of a setting.

It is important to remember that a setting can offset and enhance the beauty of your diamond after you own it. While you're shopping, however, it can cover up flaws that should mean a lower price. We'll discuss how to determine the design and value of your setting in a later chapter on gold.

I'm sorry to report how many people have told me that they bought a diamond because they liked the setting it was in. Usually for stones of 1/4 ct. and up, the diamond's value can be double, triple that of the gold. *After* you have decided on the best shape and then on the best stone, you should begin looking for a setting that really does it justice.

From Octahedron to Diamond

Let us begin "cut" by explaining how a diamond gets its shape. If you ever wondered why a baseball diamond or a jack of diamonds is shaped the way it is, it is because classic diamonds in the rough have that "diamond" shape.

This shape is an octahedron, and is an eight-sided figure built like two pyramids, one inverted on top of the other. (See illustration #3.)

Rough diamond

Illustration 3

—— *Well-cut stone*
--- *Poorly-cut stone*

Although diamonds are the hardest natural substance and can't be scratched by anything but another diamond, they have a crystalline structure and can be broken. In fact, like wood, they have a discernible grain. Just like a log is split on the grain, diamonds are often "cleaved," or split in two, by striking them on the grain. The two parts are then polished to the form you see in jewelry stores.

The modern diamond cutter usually cuts two diamonds out of a rough stone. As you can see, the largest possible shape from a rough will usually be a round brilliant diamond.

Many rough diamond crystals are shaped in various odd shapes so that the best yield can only be produced in each case by cutting certain shapes. Therefore, a cutter doesn't get up in the morning and say to himself while yawning, "Oh! What shape do I feel like cutting today?" Rather, he carefully studies the rough and determines which shape and cut will yield the greatest carat weight with the cleanest, clearest stone. That decision will determine the shape of the diamond.

Contrary to what many salesmen tell their customers, for the most part fancy shapes (that is anything but round) are less expensive than rounds. Bear in mind that the market is forever changing and some shapes vary in popularity, causing changes in supply and demand and, ultimately, changes in price. Twenty-five years ago, in some circles, if you didn't have an emerald cut you didn't have a diamond. Five years ago, you almost couldn't give away an emerald cut diamond.

Today, the marquise and pear shape cut are the rage. Marquise diamonds of 3/4 ct. to 1 ct. are difficult to find on the market and command a premium price. Pear shapes and even emerald cuts are much more in demand than even one year ago.

Of course, supply and demand affects the market and, as of today, marquises and rounds are generally about the same price at the top of the market. This means these cuts generally command a higher price than diamonds of the same weight cut differently. Other fancy shapes trail from 10 percent to 25 percent less in value.

Just as with every other aspect of a diamond purchase, I believe you should *not* purchase a marquise or a round shape just because they are generally more popular, but rather you should purchase what you like and feel comfortable with. My rule is: know what you want, know what the market is, and pay within the market price!

The Quality of the Cut

Diamonds have captivated men and women for hundreds of years due to their fiery beauty. This optical miracle is due to diamonds' qualities of reflecting and refracting light. Every properly cut diamond has fifty-eight facets that can capture light and sparkle through a complex series of reflections and the diamond's high rate of refraction. A well cut or at least reasonably well cut diamond will show off these qualities and all of the facets. In a poorly cut stone, light will leak out rather than contribute to the brilliance (see illustration #4).

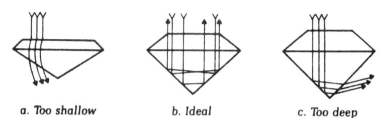

a. Too shallow   b. Ideal   c. Too deep

Illustration 4: Poorly cut diamonds lose light instead of reflecting it.

After deciding which shape you would prefer to purchase, it is very important to consider the quality of the cut of the diamond. Diamonds that are cut within certain dimensions will be brighter, much more beautiful and hence more valuable. Diamonds that are cut poorly will be worth less.

It is not uncommon for a diamond merchant to push color and clarity and almost disregard the quality of the cut. This sometimes results in the purchase of a diamond that is really worth 20, 30, or 40 percent less than what the merchant is charging you, just because of the poor cut.

Judging the Cut

In judging the basic cut of a diamond, there are a few simple areas to pay attention to. While these apply mainly to round brilliant diamonds they can be adapted to other shapes as well. As we said, in order to look at these factors properly you will need to view the diamonds loose and in natural light. Any dealer who has not made provisions for you to view diamonds loose is not interested in selling to the educated consumer.

The Table

First look at the diamond from the top. The large flat section at the top of the diamond is called the table (see illustration #5). The table reflects white light. It is like a very powerful mirror. To the sides of the table are the facets.

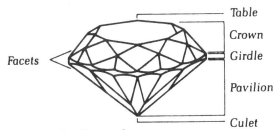

Illustration 5: Parts of a diamond

The facets work as a prism and break up the light into its colors and give the diamond its sparkle or scintillation. If a table is too large and there is too much white light but not enough sparkle, the diamond looks dull. If the table is much too small and there is too much faceting, the diamond also does not seem to jump out at you with brilliance. We're looking for balance.

Industry accepted standards are that a 53 percent table is ideal. That means that the size of table is 53 percent of the diameter of the stone (see illustration #6). All percentages in a diamond are based on the ratio of that measurement relative to the diameter. In general, a good sized table on a diamond ranges anywhere from 58 percent to 64 percent.

To judge this measurement without using special tools, there is a simple visual trick. Looking at the top of the diamond, you will see that its table shows up as a square (see illustration #7). When the square bows in slightly, it is generally an excellent size table. When the square

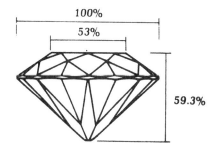

Illustration 6: Ideal diamond proportions

is exactly even, it is still considered a good table, probably still under the 64 percent range. When the table bows out and it looks some what like a cushion or pillow, it is usually over 64 percent or 65 percent. This is not considered within good or reasonable dimensions.

The Depth

Judging the depth of a diamond is a bit more difficult. It should suffice to get a good look at the diamond from the side and compare it with our diagram of a well cut diamond. Is the upper part of the diamond or crown much too heavy or chunky? Is it much too shallow or almost non-existent? Either of these would not be good.

Is the pavilion or the bottom of the diamond much too deep or much too shallow? That is also not good. The

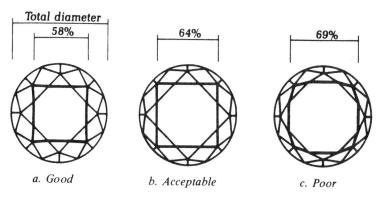

a. Good   b. Acceptable   c. Poor

Illustration 7: Table proportions

overall depth, that being the crown and the pavilion together, should be somewhere in between 58 percent and 61 percent of the diameter. Jewelers do have tools to measure this and can easily show you how to figure depth percentage (see illustration #8). You can measure the total depth of the stone and divide it by the diameter of the stone to determine the depth percentage and if the depth is within the proper range.

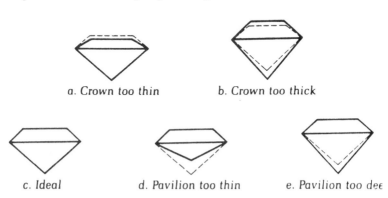

a. Crown too thin   b. Crown too thick

c. Ideal   d. Pavilion too thin   e. Pavilion too dee

Illustration 8: Depth proportions

It usually suffices to make a mental note of the shape of the stone from the side and transpose it in your mind on to a diagram of a perfect diamond. Better yet, bring the book along. It lets the salesperson know you are a conscientious shopper. If it looks much, much different, beware!

The Girdle

Next, it is important to take a fairly close look at the edge, or the girdle, of the diamond. To do that, you may want to put the diamond down on its table or top and place both sides of the tweezers around the standing bottom half of the diamond. (See illustration #9A.) This is not difficult to do if you have the diamond on a cloth. A diamond cloth should always be available to clean the diamond before examining it. You'd be amazed how many "flaws" can be erased with a good cloth.

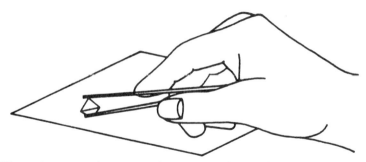

Illustration 9a: Picking up and inspecting diamond

Hold the tweezers in your left hand between your thumb and middle finger and leave your forefinger up in the air. Spin the diamond with this finger and examine the entire girdle (illustration #9B). An extremely thick edge is a sign of a diamond which was cut too heavy and appears smaller than it should for its weight. This is generally to be avoided because a thick girdle is a waste of diamond. (I have the same problem. I'm not overweight, I'm really 6 ft-4 inches in a 5 ft-9 inch body. You see, I'm not overweight, I'm just short for my height? Think about it!)

A medium girdle is the best. Slightly thinner or slightly thicker is also okay. Check for consistency of width to determine whether it is the same thickness all the way around.

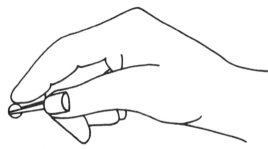

Illustration 9b: Looking at the diamond girdle

Please avoid what we call a "knife edge" girdle. This is a diamond with a girdle literally as thin as a knife's edge. A stone with a knife edge girdle is very brittle in the girdle area. After a period of time, you rarely find a diamond with a knife edge girdle that has not been chipped. Sometimes, it can break severely. I personally would rather own a diamond with a thick girdle than a diamond with a knife edge girdle. (See illustration #10.)

a. Knife Edge   *b. Thin*   *c. Medium*   *d. Heavy*

Illustration 10

Symmetry

In general, after getting a good look at the table, general depth, crown, pavilion and the girdle, the last thing to get a good look at is the diamond's basic symmetry, or evenness. Is the stone round? Are the facets lopsided? Are there any flat sides? Is the point or culet in the center or over to one side? (See illustration #11.)

Illustration 11: Poor symmetry, off-center culet, asymmetric table

Any aspect of the cut that varies from a harmonious. well proportioned diamond may lower the objective market value of the stone.

Diamond Cutting Proportions

To explain why diamonds are cut differently, let us begin by making a simple analogy between the butcher and the diamond cutter. The butcher and the diamond cutter, when they begin to prepare their ground beef or cut their diamonds, have the same motivation: profit.

Let's take the butcher first. In your ground beef, you the consumer would like to see all beef and no fat. Beef costs money and fat is cheap. The butcher on the other hand, makes more profit according to how much fat per pound he can get away with.

Some butchers will try to pull the wool over their customers' eyes and push the fat in ground beef to the limit. Some people will buy it, some people won't. Other butchers would prefer to charge more per pound and promote their lean ground beef. Of course, you have butchers that come in between.

Now let's look at the diamond cutter. A perfect cut produces a smaller yield in carat weight — similar to the pure lean meat. At the other extreme, a very poorly cut diamond may weigh more but will lack the beautiful reflective and refractive qualities that give a diamond its unique appeal.

In 1919, a scientist named Marcelles Tolkowski developed the "perfect" or "ideal" cut diamond. This cut has dimensions that display the diamond's maximum optical qualities. Today very few, if any, cutters cut those exact dimensions. Many cutters would prefer to cut good, but not quite perfect, dimensions (refer to illustration #6 on page 20).

Although some diamond dealers will try to tell you that perfect cuts on diamonds command tremendous premiums at resale, that is simply not factual. A perfect cut is worth slightly more than a fine cut but reasonable dimensions are sufficient to show off the beauty of the diamond and command top dollar.

Somewhere between perfect cut and poorly cut is a cut which balances between optimal beauty and weight. The result is full of fiery sparkle and yet maximizes the value. This type of stone is "reasonably well cut," which is all the market demands.

"Cheating on the Cut": Two Common Examples

I am familiar with one very large cutting firm from whom I intentionally buy very few diamonds. Based just on color and clarity, this company sells its diamonds at generally 20 percent below any of their competitors, with better payout terms.

The problem with their diamonds is that they are cut either extremely heavy, or extremely shallow. This firm is able to retain on the average at least 20 percent more weight from the rough diamond for the same polished stone by cutting in this manner.

Heavy Girdle or Edge

Unfortunately, most of the added weight is often retained in the girdle area and the actual appearance of the diamond from the top is that of a much smaller and lighter diamond. For instance, instead of cutting a .75 ct. with a thin girdle and good dimensions, this firm prefers to cut the 1.00 ct. diamond and leave in 25 percent "fat." This leaves the diamond with a heavy girdle (refer to illustration #8 on page 21).

Of course, as we explained earlier, a one carat diamond is more valuable than a three quarter carat of the same quality, by as much as 50 percent per carat. This theoretically gives the firm not only the 20 percent more weight, but pushes a diamond into the next price weight category, past the next "magic number."

In reality, though, the value of that stone is based on what the stone would weigh if it had been cut to the proper dimensions. That would be the value of a .75 carat diamond. This is the information that your average jewelry salesperson may not tell you if they have this type of stone for sale. I assure you there is an abundance of this material in the marketplace.

Shallow Cut or Swindled Diamond

The other extreme in cheating on diamond cutting is equally damaging. If the rough is broader, in order to cut a heavier stone, many cutters will cut the stone with larger horizontal measurements. The result is a wider but "shallow" or "swindled" diamond. The value of this "spread" diamond would also be based on what it would weigh if properly recut.

The advantage of this stone is a bigger looking stone that really weighs less. This lighter diamond would have the illusion of a heavier stone. The disadvantage, quite often, is a stone that lacks brilliance because of light leaking out the back and sides and not reflecting up through the top.

If one is aware of that and prefers a larger looking stone, that can be an advantage — as long as you know what it is, what it is worth, and what you are paying for it. If you like it, that's fine, but know what you are buying.

Recutting a Stone

Many people are not aware that a diamond can be recut. This is usually done to correct the dimensions of a less scientifically cut or improperly cut diamond.

Old Cuts

Does the stone look overly heavy from the side of the crown? Does it look like there is a hole in the middle of the stone when you look from the top? The hole means it has an open culet or a very large facet on the tip of the pavilion. If so, you may be looking at an "old cut" diamond.

One should be careful not to accept old cut diamonds, either an Old-Mine Cut or an Old European Cut, at full price for the same weight in modern cut. These diamonds are based on diamond cutting proportional systems used previous to Tolkowski's scientific round brilliant diamond cutting system. Old cut diamonds are less valuable than the same weight stone cut in the modern system. (See illustration #12.)

Don't be afraid to question if it is or is not a modern cut stone. An old cut stone, generally speaking, will be valued at what weight it will be when recut into modern dimensions. Therefore a 1.00 ct. old cut may be the

| a. Old European Cut | b. Old-Mine Cut |

Illustration 12

equivalent in value of a .75 ct. modern cut diamond, depending on the shape it was recut to.

This does not mean I recommend against buying antique jewelry. Antique jewelry, like all antiques, can command a high resale price and have great aesthetic appeal as a total piece of jewelry. I am referring here to the market value of the stones if you choose to remove them from their antique settings. This value is based on recutting to modern proportions.

Fancy Shapes

When it comes to fancy shapes, the same method of evaluating the cut holds true. It's a lot more difficult to tell the size of a table on a marquise or a pear, but you still want to make sure that the stone is not too shallow, which is very common in pears, marquises, and ovals. In fact, if the cut gets much too shallow in these stones, you can almost see through them. A general approach is to look at the stone in the same way as a round diamond: the table, the depth, and symmetry and the brilliance.

One area you should beware of, with regard to fancy shapes, is the appearance of a "bow tie". In a marquise or pear shape, even in a well cut stone, you generally have a small dark area shaped like a bow tie in the center of the stone.

In a very well cut stone, a bow tie is hardly noticeable. In a poorly cut stone, it can actually be very dark, gray and quite noticeable. This will, of course, interfere with the brilliance and beauty of the diamond (see illustration #13).

Illustration 13: Bow ties

As far as the quality of the shape in fancy cut diamonds, a lot of it really boils down to personal taste. In a pear shape, I personally prefer a longer spear-like pear shape. Some people prefer them almost squatty and, of course, the classic pear is somewhere in between.

In the marquise shape, some people prefer cuts which are long and slender, while other people prefer them a little bit more in the shape of a football. Some people like long emerald cuts; other people prefer them almost square. Make sure the shape is to your liking. I suggest you compare a few shapes so you can get a feel for what is available and what you find pleasing.

Don't Undercut the Cut

Ultimately, if you are looking at two diamonds that are similar and one seems a lot more brilliant than the other, assuming the colors and the clarities are about the same, you will inevitably find that their cuts are different and that is why they look different. Don't be bashful. Ask questions. Do as much comparison shopping as possible, and don't let anybody "undercut the cut."

CHAPTER 4
Color: The Third C

There is no question that the two initial Cs are carat weight and cut. Without assessing these two basic Cs — the size and shape type of the stone you want — you really cannot take the next step in choosing a diamond.

Concerning color and clarity, the next two Cs, I prefer to begin with color. This is a personal preference. For me, the color of the diamond is more important than the clarity, because this is ultimately what people see. Rarely do people walk around with loupes (magnifiers) in their eyes to magnify and see what is in the diamond. The color is what their eyes will pick up immediately.

Diamonds come in all different colors. In nature there are brown, green, blue and even some pink and extremely rare red diamonds. For the most part, however, diamonds range from what we will call colorless or white diamonds to shades of yellow. We will explain the color and clarity grading system based on the Gemological Institute of American (GIA) grading systems.

The GIA has been successful in giving the diamond industry somewhat of an objective system with which to judge and grade diamonds. Diamond grading is not an exact science, however. It is not uncommon for a person to send the stone to be graded by the GIA (which is considered the authority in this industry) and have it graded one color one time and another a second time. Even two graders in the same lab can see colors slightly differently. The reason this is so important is that color affects value and price. But those differences are slight and what usually matters most to you is getting close to the exact range of color for determining price.

Many diamond salespeople will want you to believe that an untrained eye cannot tell the subtle differences in color. But if you will follow my instructions, you will definitely be able to purchase a diamond with the confidence of knowing what its basic color is.

The GIA color grading scale starts with a D color (see illustration #14) for the top, or whitest, color and goes down in the alphabet indicating increasingly yellower colors until it reaches Z. Beyond that are fancy yellow or "canary" colored stones. There are no A, B, or C color grades.

Illustration 14: GIA color grading scale

The GIA breaks down the beginning colors into categories that are important to understand. D, E and F are considered colorless, G, H, I, and J near colorless, and K, L, and M colors beginning in the faint yellow range. Colors beyond that point get into generally less desirable yellows until one reaches the fancy yellow range. Prices will continue to drop slightly.

The way to judge the color of a diamond is to always see the diamond unmounted or loose. It is unwise to ever buy a diamond of any significance in a mounting. As I mentioned before, the mounting impacts your judgment of the cut of the stone; but it is also impossible to see accurate color through the mounting. Many stores specifically mount their stones in order to cover up the color.

When judging the color of a diamond, it is important to see the diamond in good natural light or, at worst, under cool white fluorescent lights. The GIA also sells a light box that is very effective for color grading.

Most jewelry stores have very strong lighting that specifically distorts the color and makes everything look

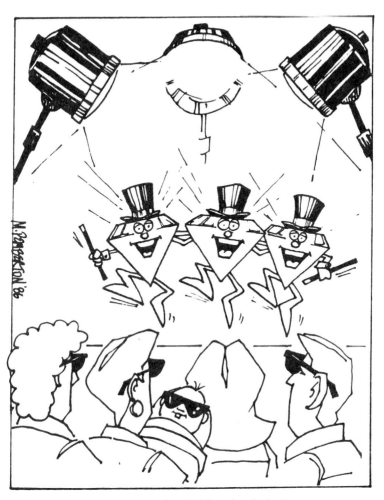

"Don't be blinded by the light."

similar. The strong spotlight type lights that most jewelry stores have are there to confuse you, and not to help you in judging the color of the diamond.

Providing the proper light may be a problem for stores that do not have adequate lighting, but I am sorry to say that I cannot sanction buying a diamond without seeing it in good light. All stores have the option of providing a GIA light box. When enough people demand proper lighting in order to purchase their diamonds, these stores will change.

The loose diamond should be shown against a pure white background, preferably in a professional diamond grading tray. Except for diamonds with really distinct colors, a well cut diamond mounted in white or yellow gold will appear whiter than it is and may look as good as G-H color (see illustration #15).

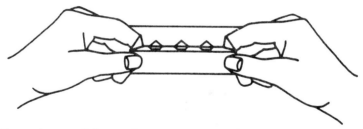

Illustration 15: Color grading tray

Unfortunately, I know this to be a fact based on my own experience. I have bought mounted diamonds more than once when I was sure that the color was much better than it really was. When I took it out of the mounting, I was in for a surprise! That can really hurt the pocket book. Interestingly enough, if a diamond is cut well enough to display its full reflective qualities, even an L, M or an N color diamond may "face up" (or appear on the surface in a setting) extremely white.

When judging color, place the diamond upside down in the color grading tray. Look at the diamond from the side as if you were looking at a cross-section. Try to

32

concentrate on the color of the diamond at the girdle or the edge of the diamond. That is because this is the thinnest part of the diamond with the least mass. When judging or comparing two diamonds, especially if they are of different sizes, looking into the dense center of the stone (where the mass may be greater in one) may distort the comparison. Therefore, the best areas for comparison are on the edge or the girdle of the stone.

If a diamond placed against a white background has literally no yellow cast or tinge whatsoever, it is probably in the D, E, or F color range. The difference between a D, E, or F is the transparency of the stone. D stones are not only colorless; they are also extremely transparent and crystal clear. If the diamond has just the slightest tint, but is still extremely white when you turn it right side up, it is in the G, H, or possibly the I, or J range.

Actually, to substantiate the color of a diamond one should request to compare the color with that of a diamond that has a GIA certificate. Make sure the jeweler proves that the certified stone matches the certificate. Don't be surprised if your jewelry dealer doesn't have any certified stones. Many will insist that the grading is subjective and inconsistent. While there is some variability in grading, my view is that it's much better than nothing. It will bring the value of a diamond as close in range as is possible.

In fact, there is an industry tool known as a "CZ grading set." These are cubic zirconia, synthetic diamond substitutes which are laboratory graded for color. They are relatively inexpensive but are not currently available to the public. This is an unfortunate situation I am working on correcting because with such a set the consumer could be much more confident about color grading. Until such sets reach the consumer at a reasonable price, it remains your jewelry salesperson's obligation to prove the color of any stone.

In good light with a good white background — even without color grading stones — it is not difficult to get into the basic color range of the stone. Always ask yourself, "Is the stone colorless?" If it literally has no color, you know that you have got to be somewhere in the D, E, F, or G range. An H color will have an oh so slight bit of color.

Ask yourself, "Does the stone have a very signficant tint to it?" "Is it starting to get too yellow?" If so, you know you are probably in the L, M, or N range or lower. "Is the yellow extremely minor?" Maybe it is an I or maybe it's a J, possibly a K. The more you look at stones, the easier it will be to judge them without a grade stone.

With research for this book as motivation, I recently canvassed larger chain stores at one of the major shopping malls in my area. I went around looking for a one carat diamond. Practically no one was able to show me diamonds in proper light. One branch of a leading chain store offered me what they represented as a very high clarity, G color, 1.50 ct. for what I thought was an extremely reasonable price. The problems were that they didn't have proper lighting available for me to examine the color of the diamond, and that the stone was mounted.

I told the manager that I would like to see the stone in good light. The best he could do was to take me into the center of the mall under a skylight, which was "semi-decent" lighting.

Against a white background with the stone turned upside down, in the mounting, it was apparent that this diamond had a light yellow cast. Although it was only a tint, it nevertheless was probably no better than a K color, and quite possibly worse. As a G color diamond, this would have been a real honest-to-goodness bargain at a wholesale price. As a K color diamond, the price was high, and really way out of line.

The difference in value was literally thousands of dollars, and there was no way this company would substantiate or guarantee the grade of the stone. This story emphasizes the importance of color grading only loose diamonds in good light, upside down, and against a white background. With these conditions, you should be able to get a very good idea of the diamond's color range.

Don't "make light" of the quality of the light you are using to make sure you are not getting a horse or a stone of a different color than the one you bargained for.

Certificate Diamonds

In diamond grading, only carat weight and cut are truly objectively measurable. Now that we are beginning to discuss the more subjective qualities, color and clarity, we should explain the advantages and disadvantages of certificate diamonds.

A certificate diamond is a diamond that has been graded by a gemological laboratory that has determined the diamond's 4 Cs grading for you. As mentioned previously, the purpose of this guide is to make you an educated customer, possessing the tools and the guts to judge diamonds by and for yourself and to teach you that you need not be totally dependent on someone else's grading. This is important because some diamond sellers do not represent their product honestly.

Unfortunately, this also holds true with many gemological laboratories. The laboratory's customer may influence the judgment of the diamond grader. After all, the laboratory makes its living by taking money for this service, and keeping its customers, the diamond sellers, happy is only natural. Laboratories are also not infallible. Therefore, do not rely solely on a certificate. Always check it out yourself. By far, the GIA is the most reliable respected certification, but the GIA is not beyond making an error in grading.

On the other hand, when you get to expensive diamonds of very high grades, a GIA certificate carries "clout", and is well advised. Some jewelers dismiss certificates as irrelevant, some rely on them as gospel. My opinion about certificates is somewhere between the two extremes. I use them as just another tool to help me determine the value of any specific diamond.

Other Colors

Just a few more helpful hints on colors. The basic colors in diamonds, as we mentioned earlier, range from white to yellows, but there is a tremendous variety of colors that appear in natural diamonds. Rare colors such as blue and pink or very intense yellow become very expensive stones and are very specialized. Generally speaking, real blues and real pinks are rare and will probably sell at a higher price than fine whites. Fine intense yellow or canary colors can also get costly.

There are also other colors in diamonds that are quite prevalent and quite plentiful. It is not uncommon for a vendor or a merchant to try to sell a brown diamond at a premium on the market. Brown, black or gray diamonds are not expensive items. Quite often the true color of certain diamonds will be questionable. Browns and pinks for instance, are closely related but browns are inexpensive and pinks are out of sight.

When getting into diamonds of significant value, it is probably a good suggestion that the GIA determine the real color. When being sold a diamond that has a certificate from the GIA, always remember that the second color listed is the primary color. For instance, if a certificate reads pinkish-brown, that is definitely not as impressive as a brownish-pink. A bluish-gray does not come close in rarity and value to grayish-blue.

Diamonds that have naturally undesirable color are often artificially treated to intensify and change their color. For instance, it is not uncommon to find treated blues, treated greens, and even treated browns. Of course, intense yellow or "canary" diamonds can also be treated to achieve the canary yellow. The treatment is irradiation and, as you might guess, early experiments with irradiating diamonds to affect their color resulted in radioactive stones. Most of them, thankfully are not in circulation at this point. Today's irradiated stones are quite safe.

It is not always apparent that a diamond is treated, even to a trained jeweler. When a lot of money is involved with the purchase of a diamond in any of these specialized colors, let the GIA check out the authenticity and determine the real color.

CHAPTER 5
Clarity: The Fourth C

By definition, clarity grading is the determination of the flaws or inclusions in a diamond. When a diamond is formed, if the crystals form at perfect angles and if there is no foreign matter present, then the diamond is pure of inclusions or flaws.

If, however, the crystals did not form at perfect angles in relationship to one another, the result could be internal cracks, "feathers," cleavages or other flaws. Black or other color marks in diamonds are often caused by the diamond forming around other minerals.

A useful parallel to this process is the formation of ice. Placing the same tap water in an icecube tray will produce some cubes with air bubbles, others with flaws like cracks and feathers and some perfectly clear cubes.

When judging the clarity of a diamond, as far as the value of the diamond is concerned, it doesn't really make a difference what type of flaw or inclusion is in the stone. What really matters is how the flaw affects the beauty of the diamond. An exception is if the flaw affects the durability of the stone — such as a severe crack or break in the stone, or a chip on the edge.

Using the Loupe

Diamonds are judged at 10X magnification. This is an international convention. When the GIA studies a diamond, they study it under a microscope at 10X. Most diamond dealers will use a loupe, which is a professional corrected lens made for studying diamonds and gemstones. For these loupes, again, 10X is the regulation.

People will often study diamonds at higher powers to see what they can find; but ultimately the magnification is brought back to 10X to see if there is anything visible at that standard magnification.

One of the most important keys to correctly judging clarity is being able to use a loupe, and use it properly. It is not uncommon for diamond salespeople to base their grading on what they think the customer can see or cannot see. Therefore, you must know how to get the accurate view of the diamond. Try to be comfortable with the tweezers that hold the diamond up to the loupe. Relax! Contrary to popular belief, you won't hurt the diamond. The dealer may not want you to be too comfortable — you'll see too much!

With a minimum amount of practice, you can see just about anything the trained eye can see. On more than one occasion, I've shown my customers diamonds, and using the loupe they've discovered inclusions that I did not notice.

The efficient way to use a loupe is to hold it about one to two inches from your eye (see illustration #16). Bring the diamond tweezers almost up to the lens and then move it slowly away from the loupe until it focuses. Be sure to brace one hand up against the other in some comfortable fashion. This will steady the loupe and afford you clear vision of the diamond.

Move the diamond back and forth and study it from all angles. *Take your time!* Don't be rushed. After a few times at the loupe, you should be quite comfortable. Make sure the diamond is clean and free of dust or finger prints. Don't be shy! Question everything foreign that you see.

When holding the diamond in the tweezers, be as relaxed as possible. Don't squeeze too hard — you may pop it right out of the tweezers. If it falls, nothing to worry about. Just pick it right back up. To do so, make sure the diamond is flat with its table side down, put the tweezers flat against the table and squeeze gently. To turn the diamond over, just get one end of the tweezer under

Illustration 16: Using the loupe

it and gently flip. It's easy; just practice a bit, and you'll be a pro.

Many merchants have microscopes. They are helpful in many ways to provide a better view of the diamond with better lighting. The problem with the scope is really being able to see the stone from all angles and being allowed to focus properly by yourself. I therefore recommend getting used to a loupe.

The advantage of the loupe is that you can carry it in your pocket, and use it anywhere. Try that with a microscope! Most jewelers will have a loupe available to use if you ask. Make sure it's a 10X corrected lens.

The GIA Grading Scale

Let's work backward from the right of the chart. (See illustration #17.) The last three grades are Imperfect 1-2-3. The definition of an "Imperfect" diamond is one that has flaws that are visible to the naked eye. I generally tell my customers that if you can see the flaws from across the room, it's an Imperfect 3 (I_3). If you can see the flaws from a distance like 18 inches, it's an Imperfect

2 (I_2). If you can see the flaw just barely at a close distance, it is an I_1. Technically, the stone can be Imperfect 1 (I_1) if it has a great number of flaws, even if they are not visible to the naked eye. For purposes of price evaluation, for the most part we will consider "eye clean" as just above Imperfect 1 (I_1) or in the slight imperfection category.

Illustration 17: GIA clarity scale

If its flaws are not eye visible, but when you "loupe" the diamond the flaws are significant and almost jump out at you, the diamond is an SI_1 or SI_2. SI stands for "Slight Imperfections," and the imperfections should be easily visible to *anyone* under 10X magnification.

If they are really bad flaws, by virtue of their size, darkness and number, the stone would be graded an SI_2 clarity. For example, if there are a fair number of medium-sized flaws or just one heavy dark flaw located in the center, this would mar the beauty of the diamond significantly, and be graded an SI_2. If the imperfections are easily visible under the loupe, but not that severe, it would be graded SI_1.

Sometimes a cutter will improve on a "dark flaw" by "lasering" the diamond. This means he will drill a minute hole with a laser beam and dissolve the dark spot with acids forced through the channel. This will leave a white flaw but will also leave a "drill hole." This would still be at least an SI_2.

A diamond that is categorized a VS stone, or "Very Slight Imperfections" means imperfections that are much less significant in terms of damaging the beauty of the diamond. If you loupe the diamond and initially see no inclusions, and as you study it small inclusions begin to appear, this is probably a VS stone.

A VS$_2$ may have a few small flaws or one in the center. A VS1 would have maybe one small one on the side.

A true VVS diamond, or "Very, Very Slight Imperfection", should usually be clean when louped. If I *cannot* find anything with the loupe, my assumption is it is probably a VVS diamond. However, to really grade a true VVS diamond in a fine color grade, a GIA certificate is usually advisable to give it clout. A real VVS diamond is quite immaculate.

By the same principle, I would never take the responsibility of calling a diamond Flawless without a GIA certificate. That is a statement only a recognized authority can make with any credibility.

Certification and Value

Ultimately, clarity grading is very subjective and no two graders will necessarily grade exactly alike. This guide will not make you an expert grader in terms of being extremely accurate on every grade, but you will have enough information to get close.

Both in clarity and color grading, when we are talking in terms of a D color or a flawless stone at the top of the line or close to these grades, I highly recommend that you only purchase with a GIA certificate. When talking about more common grades or even slightly finer stones, it is only important to get within a close range in order to really evaluate the buy.

I was asked to appraise a stone for sale in a divorce settlement by a women whose husband had assured her it was a high value stone. Since I never rely on my grading to call a stone a D flawless, I appraised it at a price for a D-VVS.

The next day her husband angrily confronted me with a GIA certificate for a flawless stone, and I promptly reappraised the stone appropriately. That certificate was worth several thousand dollars at resale. While I consider myself a good diamond grader, I didn't feel I had the clout to appraise at that grade without the GIA backing me.

We should note that laboratories charge a fee for their grading. You should be sure to consider the relative value of the certificate to the cost of the stone.

Grading for Yourself

To reiterate, always look at the stone carefully without a loupe before magnifying the diamond. If you can see those imperfections with the naked eye, you know that it is basically an Imperfect diamond. How imperfect depends on how severe it looks. If the flaw is almost negligible to the naked eye, you have an Imperfect 1. If the flaws are incredibly horrendous, it could be an Imperfect 3. If it's in between, it's an Imperfect 2. By the way, what is the opposite of the "naked eye?" I guess it's a clothed eye. No, I don't lisp!

What if the stone is extremely clean? If, as you sit there and study it you have a very difficult time finding anything in the diamond, it may be VVS, or probably a fine VS. Are there some very small minute items hard to see but detectable nevertheless? Maybe it is a VS_2. It may be graded SI_1 by a different grader, but you've come close.

After looking at a number of stones and getting used to these basic methods, you should be able to determine the basic clarity grade of a diamond. You should at least be able to see past a salesperson who is telling you they want to sell you a VVS when it is really significantly flawed. You'll know that you'd better move on if you want an honest deal.

Know What You're Getting

I often kid my engaged customers when looking at minor flaws in a diamond that may interest them, asking them both whether or not they see each other as "flawless." The answer is usually, "Of course not," but they both want to know the "flaws" before the marriage — not after. The same holds true for diamonds. Know what you are really getting, and what it's really worth.

Again, there is no such thing as a good diamond or a bad diamond. If you're comfortable with an Imperfect stone, that's fine, at the right price. If you only feel comfortable if the stone is nearly perfect, also fine!

I vividly remember selling a 10 carat diamond that was an Imperfect 1, to a gentleman who wanted to impress his business associates and wanted to look like a "million dollars." He was a Texas oilman, and he basically wanted "lotsa flash for a little cash."

That same week, I sold a 2 carat E color VVS, to a gentleman who developed navigational equipment for the aerospace industry. As a man who did very precise work, his personality and preference dictated near perfection. Both gentlemen got what they needed to make them happy at the right price.

Along the same lines, it is generally accepted that diamonds for earrings need not be of a high clarity grade because if you're close enough to really see them, your eyes are usually closed anyway! (Cute — but true.)

Buy what you like and what you need — not what the merchant is pushing that week. And by the way, by all means — **enjoy!**

CHAPTER 6

Cost: The Fifth C

Congratulations! You've arrived! With the information in the preceding chapters under your belt, you have now reached the point where you can determine the grades of diamonds that you are looking at. Let's run through an example.

Let's assume you've been looking for 1 ct. round diamonds. A jeweler has shown you a 1.10 ct. stone. You studied it carefully and you are following the Cs step by step in your mind.

First you are analyzing the carat weight. It's over the carat, which is good. It's only a little on the heavy side — not enough for a price break, but the added weight will add 10% to the cost of the stone. That's not so bad.

Now, how does the cut look? Let's imagine that the cut looks pretty good. The table bows in a little, the side view looks respectable. The girdle may be just a bit thick, but well within reason. The stone shows its weight nicely and it really sparkles.

Now to the color. The jeweler shows it to you in good light, in a grading tray next to a proven GIA certified "G" color grading stone. He says it's a "G." It seems to you a little "yellower" but it should at least reach an H.

The clarity is next. While looking with your naked eye nothing seems to be visible. Under 10X loupe you immediately see some little specks on the edge of the stone, including a significant dark spot right on the girdle. Therefore it should be in the SI_2 range.

You now know what you're looking at. It's a slightly heavy 1 ct. diamond, reasonably cut, H color, SI$_1$ or SI$_2$. Fantastic! Now the question is, what is it worth?

To aid you in having a real market value to base your purchase on, we have provided a current price list (as of August 15, 1986) which will make all the information in this book more applicable. It is dated material which I will be happy to update if you give us a call at our shop in Denver, at (303) 534-0251. I should simply note that diamond prices were quickly rising as we went to press. Remember, this is dated material!

It is most important to understand what these prices represent and where we got them. As I've explained earlier, the confusion inherent in diamond grading has largely been cleared up by the GIA grading system, which I've explained in detail.

Democratizing the Diamond Industry

Real diamond market values traditionally were only accessible to those New York diamond dealers in close contact with the world diamond markets. Even to them, the system was largely guesswork and conjecture. Jewelers in turn had to take the New York dealers' word that their diamonds were worth what they were charging.

About eight years ago, a man named Martin Rapaport began collecting this data and publishing his opinion of diamond prices in the Rapaport Diamond Report. There has been tremendous objection to his publicizing what cutters and dealers have referred to as "inside information." There have been many unsuccessful attempts to legally prevent him from doing this. Many people claim he has been fixing prices rather than reflecting them, but the discussion is academic at this point.

The Rapaport Report has become the defacto standard among the wholesale market for pricing diamonds. His list is quoted and used in virtually all diamond markets throughout the world. Martin Rapaport has accomplished what he set out to do. He was quoted as saying "My list has democratized the diamond industry."

Of course, our list is a "wholesale plus" list. It is based somewhat on Rapaport, although I feel at times that he is not totally consistent with the real market. Therefore, I have made adjustments that reflect the market as I see it.

It is wholesale plus, since there may be several layers of dealers between the cutter and you, and the wholesale price index would be an unreasonable guide for you, the consumer. It is legitimate and fair that dealers who travel to New York, Antwerp, and Israel, maintain an inventory and salespeople, should make a profit for their trouble. Therefore, my price list reflects the wholesale plus a significant percentage. Any jeweler buying their diamonds "right," I feel should be able to sell them at these general prices.

These do not include traditional retail mark ups. You may be able to buy diamonds for less than the prices here. I consistently sell below these prices for example, or you may have to spend more, but this should provide an extremely useful guideline.

Judging the Cost

Now back to the evaluation. We were looking at a 1.10 ct. diamond. Check the chart for 1 ct. diamond. Find the coordinates for an H and an SI_2. The price lists at $3150 per carat. Multiply the $3150 x 1.10 ct. to add the value of the extra weight over 1 carat and you'll have the total value on the stone which is $3465 (see illustration #18).

Now you have an idea what a fair price from a jeweler would be. If the jeweler is offering you the diamond for $6000, I feel this price is excessive. Don't buy it. On the other hand, if he wants $3850, and you've shopped, and you like it, the price is not out of line.

You may want to offer less money. Don't be bashful. All the salesperson can say is no. If you shop you may find the stone for as low as $3000 or less.

These are some of your choices. By reading this guide, following basic instructions, and not jumping into a purchase too quickly, you should know what the dia-

1 ct: 1.00 - 1.99
(if 1.50 or more add 10%)

	IF	VVS$_1$	VVS$_2$	VS$_1$	VS$_2$	SI$_1$	SI$_2$	I$_1$	I$_2$	I$_3$
D	20000	12000	9500	6500	5800	4700	4000	2600	1800	1400
E	12000	9500	8000	5600	5500	4400	3900	2400	1700	1300
F	9500	8000	7000	5400	5000	4100	3700	2200	1700	1300
G	8000	7000	6000	5000	4500	3800	3400	2000	1600	1200
H	7000	6000	5000	4500	4000	3500	3400	2000	1600	1200
I	5000	4700	4300	3900	3500	3300	3000	1800	1500	1100
J	4000	3700	3700	3300	3100	3000	2700	1600	1400	1000
K	3300	2800	3000	2800	2700	2500	2500	1500	1300	800
L	2700	2500	2300	2400	2200	2000	1900	1400	1300	700
M	2300	2000	1900	1800	1700	1600	1500	1300	1100	600

(In the SI$_2$ column the value 3150 is circled.)

(Handwritten calculation:)

$$\frac{\$3150 \times 1.10 \text{ cts.}}{\$3465}$$

All prices are dated August 15, 1986. Please use these figures only as a point of comparison. Jay Feder assumes no liability and makes no guarantees as to the accuracy of these charts.

These prices are the author's opinion.

Illustration 18: Diamond value computation

mond is, what it is worth, and what kind of deal you are getting. You may not be an expert yet but you *are* an informed consumer. Pretty good feeling, huh?

CHAPTER 7

Determining Market Value: The Price Charts

Before we begin, let me reiterate that the diamond market is constantly changing. These price charts, listed in the appendix, are dated as of August 15, 1986. Nevertheless, I believe they are still helpful. Updates will be available at a later date in a newsletter we plan to publish.

How to Use the Price Charts

1. Find the carat size. Determine the color and clarity of the diamond.
2. Follow the color on the horizontal and the clarity on the vertical and find the price per carat where they meet. (If the diamond seems in between colors and clarities, determine the worst it could be or at least no better than half way between). If the best it could be is $2200 per carat and the worst is $1800 per carat, figure $2000. Prices will continue to get somewhat lower as you continue past M color towards fancy yellow, but not tremendously.
3. Multiply the per carat price times the weight of the diamond.
4. Carat Weight — Most off sizes are covered in separate charts, but you can deduct 5% for "weird" sizes such as 1.22 ct. or .71 ct. Don't forget to add 10-15 percent for each ½ ct. size and up such as 1.50 ct.+, 2.50 ct+, etc. This means that if the chart lists the price for a 1 ct. at $3100, a 1.50 carat stone or larger is worth 10-15 percent more money. Review the chapter

on carat weight for the list and explanation of magic numbers used as a standard here.

5. Cut — Market popularity of different cuts changes often. As of this printing, you may have to add up to 10 percent for marquise shapes. Pear shapes may be minus 5 percent. Deduct 10 percent for ovals, emeralds, and radiants, 15-25 percent for heart shapes. Deduct 5-20 percent for poor cuts. Subtract 5-15 percent for minor problems such as thick girdle or off round. You'll need 25 percent for extremely "heavy" or shallow stones that should really be recut smaller to be presentable. You may have to add up to 10 percent for an extremely fine cut.

Now make your calculations and DEAL. If jewelry salespeople disagree with your calculations, let them prove their side! Have fun!

This list does not reflect current market prices. For updated diamond and gem prices please call . . . 1-800-841-SAVE or in Denver, 534-0251.

1/3 ct: .29 - .37 ct: 29 - 37 points

	IF	VVS$_1$	VVS$_2$	VS$_1$	VS$_2$	SI$_1$	SI$_2$	I$_1$	I$_2$	I$_3$
D	3100	2835	2700	2500	2200	1800	1700	1400	1000	800
E	2800	2700	2505	2400	2100	1705	1600	1300	1000	800
F	2700	2565	2400	2200	2000	1600	1400	1200	900	700
G	2500	2340	2200	2000	1800	1400	1300	1100	800	700
H	2200	2000	2000	1800	1500	1300	1100	1000	800	700
I	1800	1600	1500	1300	1200	1100	1000	800	700	600
J	1600	1500	1300	1200	1100	1000	800	700	700	600
K	1400	1200	1105	1100	1000	805	700	600	600	400
L	1100	900	900	800	800	700	700	600	400	400
M	900	800	800	700	700	600	600	400	400	300

All prices are dated August 15, 1986. Please use these figures only as a point of comparison.
These prices are the author's opinion. Jay Feder assumes no liability and makes no guarantees as to the accuracy of these charts.

3/8 ct: .38 - .45 ct: 38 - 45 points

	IF	VVS₁	VVS₂	VS₁	VS₂	SI₁	SI₂	I₁	I₂	I₃
D	3700	3400	3100	2700	2600	2000	1800	1600	1200	1000
E	3305	3100	2850	2600	2300	2000	1800	1500	1200	1000
F	3100	2800	2600	2430	2200	1800	1600	1300	1000	800
G	2700	2500	2300	2200	2000	1600	1400	1300	1000	800
H	2500	2300	2200	2000	1800	1400	1300	1200	1000	800
I	2000	1900	1700	1600	1400	1300	1100	1000	800	700
J	1900	1800	1600	1500	1400	1100	1000	900	800	700
K	1700	1600	1500	1400	1200	1000	1000	900	700	600
L	1300	1200	1200	1100	1000	800	800	700	600	500
M	1100	1100	900	800	800	700	700	600	500	400

All prices are dated August 15, 1986. Please use these figures only as a point of comparison. These prices are the author's opinion. Jay Feder assumes no liability and makes no guarantees as to the accuracy of these charts.

Light Halves: .46 - .49; 46 - 49 points

	IF	VVS₁	VVS₂	VS₁	VS₂	SI₁	SI₂	I₁	I₂	I₃
D	4300	3600	3400	3100	2700	2600	2300	1900	1300	1000
E	3600	3400	3100	2700	2600	2400	2200	1800	1300	1000
F	3400	3100	2800	2600	2400	2300	2000	1600	1200	950
G	3000	2700	2500	2300	2200	2000	1800	1400	1000	950
H	2700	2500	2300	2200	2000	1800	1700	1300	1000	950
I	2200	2000	1900	1800	1600	1500	1400	1100	950	800
J	2000	1800	1700	1600	1500	1400	1200	1000	950	800
K	2000	1700	1600	1500	1400	1200	1100	1000	850	700
L	1400	1300	1300	1200	1000	950	950	850	700	600
M	1200	1000	1000	950	950	850	850	700	600	500

All prices are dated August 15, 1986. Please use these figures only as a point of comparison. These prices are the author's opinion. Jay Feder assumes no liability and makes no guarantees as to the accuracy of these charts.

1/2 ct: .50 - .69 ct: 50 - 60 points

	IF	VVS₁	VVS₂	VS₁	VS₂	SI₁	SI₂	I₁	I₂	I₃
D	6700	4900	4300	3800	3200	3000	2700	2000	1300	1100
E	4900	4300	4000	3500	3100	2800	2600	2000	1300	1100
F	4300	4000	3800	3200	3000	2700	2400	1900	1200	1100
G	3900	3700	3200	3000	2700	2500	2200	1700	1100	950
H	3600	3200	3000	2700	2600	2300	2100	1600	1100	950
I	3000	2700	2700	2400	2100	2000	1800	1400	950	800
J	2500	2200	2100	2000	1900	1800	1500	1200	950	800
K	2000	1900	1700	1600	1600	1500	1200	1100	800	700
L	1700	1600	1400	1300	1200	1100	1100	950	700	600
M	1300	1200	1200	1000	1000	950	950	800	600	500

All prices are dated August 15, 1986. Please use these figures only as a point of comparison. These prices are the author's opinion. Jay Feder assumes no liability and makes no guarantees as to the accuracy of these charts.

3/4 ct: .70 - .89 ct: 70 - 89 points

	IF	VVS$_1$	VVS$_2$	VS$_1$	VS$_2$	SI$_1$	SI$_2$	I$_1$	I$_2$	I$_3$
D	8100	5400	4900	4300	3900	3400	3100	2400	1700	1200
E	5400	4900	4400	4000	3800	3200	3000	2300	1600	1200
F	4900	4455	4000	3800	3500	3100	2800	2200	1400	1200
G	4300	3900	3600	3400	3100	2900	2600	2000	1300	1000
H	3900	3600	3400	3100	2900	2600	2300	1800	1300	1000
I	3400	3000	2900	2600	2500	2200	2000	1600	1200	950
J	2700	2600	2500	2400	2200	2000	1800	1500	1100	950
K	2400	2250	2100	2000	1900	1800	1500	1400	950	800
L	1800	1700	1700	1600	1400	1300	1200	1100	800	700
M	1700	1600	1400	1300	1300	1200	1000	950	700	600

All prices are dated August 15, 1986. Please use these figures only as a point of comparison. Jay Feder assumes no liability and makes no guarantees as to the accuracy of these charts.

These prices are the author's opinion.

Light 1 ct .90 - .95 ct: .90 - .95 points
(if .96 - .99 ct add 10%)

	IF	VVS₁	VVS₂	VS₁	VS₂	SI₁	SI₂	I₁	I₂	I₃
D	9200	6700	5800	4900	4500	3800	3400	2600	1800	1300
E	6700	5800	5100	4500	4200	3600	3200	2400	1700	1300
F	5800	5100	4700	4200	3900	3400	3100	2300	1600	1300
G	5000	4500	4100	3800	3500	3100	2900	2100	1400	1200
H	4500	4200	3900	3500	3200	2900	2600	1900	1400	1200
I	3700	3400	3100	3000	2800	2500	2200	1600	1300	1080
J	3100	2875	2700	2600	2500	2200	2000	1500	1200	1080
K	2600	2500	2400	2200	2100	1900	1700	1375	1100	950
L	2000	1920	1800	1700	1600	1400	1300	1200	1100	850
M	1800	1680	1600	1400	1400	1300	1200	1100	950	700

All prices are dated August 15, 1986. Please use these figures only as a point of comparison. These prices are the author's opinion. Jay Feder assumes no liability and makes no guarantees as to the accuracy of these charts.

1 ct: 1.00 - 1.99
(if 1.50 or more add 10%)

	IF	VVS₁	VVS₂	VS₁	VS₂	SI₁	SI₂	I₁	I₂	I₃
D	20000	12000	9500	6500	5800	4700	4000	2600	1800	1400
E	12000	9500	8000	5600	5500	4400	3900	2400	1700	1300
F	9500	8000	7000	5400	5000	4100	3700	2200	1700	1300
G	8000	7000	6000	5000	4500	3800	3400	2000	1600	1200
H	7000	6000	5000	4500	4000	3500	3150	1900	1500	1200
I	5000	4700	4300	3900	3500	3300	3000	1800	1500	1100
J	4000	3700	3700	3300	3100	3000	2700	1600	1400	1000
K	3300	2800	3000	2800	2700	2500	2500	1500	1300	800
L	2700	2500	2300	2400	2200	2000	1900	1400	1300	700
M	2300	2000	1900	1800	1700	1600	1500	1300	1100	600

All prices are dated August 15, 1986. Please use these figures only as a point of comparison.
These prices are the author's opinion. Jay Feder assumes no liability and makes no guarantees as to the accuracy of these charts.

2 ct: 2.00 - 2.90 ct
(if 2.50 ct or more add 10%)

	IF	VVS₁	VVS₂	VS₁	VS₂	SI₁	SI₂	I₁	I₂	I₃
D	23000	15000	12000	10000	8800	7100	6000	4000	2400	1700
E	15500	13000	11500	9500	8200	6700	5800	3700	2100	1700
F	13000	11500	10000	8800	7500	6300	5400	3500	2100	1700
G	11500	10000	9000	7800	6900	5800	5000	3200	2000	1600
H	10000	9500	7500	6600	6000	5200	4400	3000	1900	1600
I	7000	6000	5800	5000	4800	4400	3900	2600	1700	1500
J	5800	5200	5000	4500	4400	3900	3400	2300	1500	1300
K	4800	4400	4100	3600	3600	3200	2900	2000	1400	1200
L	3500	3100	2900	2700	2600	2400	2200	1700	1400	1100
M	3100	2600	2600	2300	2200	2000	1900	1400	1000	800

All prices are dated August 15, 1986. Please use these figures only as a point of comparison.
These prices are the author's opinion. Jay Feder assumes no liability and makes no guarantees as to the accuracy of these charts.

3 ct: (3.00 - 3.99)
(if 3.50 or more add 10%)

	IF	VVS₁	VVS₂	VS₁	VS₂	SI₁	SI₂	I₁	I₂	I₃
D	32000	24000	18000	14500	13200	10600	8400	5500	3600	2300
E	24000	18000	15500	14000	12000	10200	7900	5100	3300	2200
F	18000	15500	13500	12200	11300	9700	7400	4700	3000	2200
G	15500	13500	12000	11200	10400	9000	7000	4200	2800	2000
H	13500	12000	11500	10000	9000	7500	6500	3800	2700	1800
I	10000	9400	9200	8100	7400	6400	5400	3400	2500	1600
J	8600	8200	7500	7000	6200	5600	4800	3000	2300	1500
K	6600	6500	6000	5800	5300	4700	4300	2600	2100	1400
L	5000	4600	4500	4200	3800	3600	3300	2300	1600	1300
M	4200	3600	3500	3200	3000	2700	2500	2000	1400	1200

4.00 - 4.99 ct
(if 4.50 or more add 10%)

	IF	VVS$_1$	VVS$_2$	VS$_1$	VS$_2$	SI$_1$	SI$_2$	I$_1$	I$_2$	I$_3$
D	34000	25000	19000	16000	14100	10400	9800	6000	3600	2200
E	25000	19000	16500	15200	13000	11000	9000	5400	3200	2000
F	19000	16500	15000	13800	12300	10400	8500	5000	2900	2000
G	16500	15000	14000	12700	11500	9500	8100	4700	2600	1900
H	15000	14000	13000	11500	10200	8700	7500	4000	2400	1800
I	11000	10000	9800	9500	8800	7400	6500	3400	2300	1800
J	9400	8700	8000	7500	6500	6200	5700	3100	2200	1700
K	7500	7000	6700	6200	5800	5200	4800	2700	2100	1600
L	5200	5000	4800	4500	4200	3800	3600	2400	1900	1500
M	4300	3900	3600	3300	3100	2900	2600	2100	1600	1300

All prices are dated August 15, 1986. Please use these figures only as a point of comparison. Jay Feder assumes no liability and makes no guarantees as to the accuracy of these charts.

These prices are the author's opinion.

5 ct: 4.00 - 4.99 ct
(if 5.50 or more add 10%)

	IF	VVS$_1$	VVS$_2$	VS$_1$	VS$_2$	SI$_1$	SI$_2$	I$_1$	I$_2$	I$_3$
D	45000	31000	23000	20000	17000	15000	12000	7000	4000	2400
E	31000	23000	21000	18000	16000	13000	11000	6000	3900	2400
F	23000	21000	18000	17000	15000	13000	10000	6000	3700	2400
G	20000	18000	16000	15000	13000	11000	10000	5000	3000	2300
H	18000	16000	15000	13000	12000	10000	9000	5000	3000	2100
I	12000	12000	11000	10000	9000	8000	7000	4000	2900	2000
J	11000	10000	9000	9000	8000	7000	6000	3800	2800	2000
K	9000	8000	7500	7000	6000	6000	5000	3000	2500	1900
L	6000	6000	5400	5000	4700	4000	4000	2800	2300	1800
M	5000	4000	4000	3800	4000	3000	3000	2000	2100	1600

CHAPTER 8

Common Sense: The Sixth C

When you walk in a jewelry shop's door, the salespeople have the emotional upper hand. It is easy for them to talk about beauty, about doing something special for a loved one and showing that love by spending a lot of money. This is one particular type of sale where it is quite easy to sell the sizzle and not the steak.

Although one may say that common sense is something that you can't teach — that either you have it or you don't — I don't believe that to be totally true. When it comes to buying a diamond, I think that you can learn to have the common sense to know that we are not talking about something as inexpensive as steak, but rather about an item as expensive as a diamond.

Common sense dictates that you not be intimidated, and that you not let the sales person get the upper hand. It is imperative that you be assertive.

Do not be bashful in requiring the one who wants to sell you that diamond to show you what it is, prove to you what it is, and make a deal that is fair to both of you. You may go through the evaluation, grading and negotiation process a few times, before you're finished. **Don't be intimidated!** Salespeople need you more than you need them. You can purchase a diamond anywhere, but they need you to make their living. Let them earn it. That's the way it should be.

"Pretty good feeling, huh?"

DIAMOND BUYER'S CHECKLIST

1. CARAT WEIGHT _____
   Off Size: Yes _____ No _____

2. CUT — Shape (Circle Correct One)
   Round   Brilliant   Marquise   Pear Shape
   Emerald Cut   Heart Shape   Radiant Cut
   Other _____
   Diamond is loose, not mounted:
   Yes _____ No _____
   Table: Small _____ Medium _____
        Large _____ Too Large _____
   Depth: Too Deep (Chunky) _____ Good _____
        Reasonable _____
        Shallow (Pancake) _____
   Girdle: Too Thin (Knife Edge) _____
        Thin _____ Medium _____
        Thick _____ Very Thick _____
   Brilliance: Magnificent _____ Nice _____
        Dull or Dark _____
        Something's Very Wrong _____
   Cutlet: Small _____ Medium _____
        Large _____ Is it an old cut? _____
   Fancy Shape: Bow Tie: Hardly Noticeable _____
        Noticeable _____ Very Prominent? _____

3. COLOR — Are you viewing the diamond in good
   natural light or a light box against a white background?
   (If not, stop right there!!)   Yes _____ No _____
   If you have certified comparison grade stones: The
   diamond comes closest to _____ comparison stone.
   Without comparison grade stone: No discernible tint or
   color-colorless (D,E,F) _____
   Very, very, slight tint upside down and looks real white
   right side up (G-H) _____
   Slight tint upside down — still looks quite white right
   side up (I-J) _____

Definite light yellow (K,L,M or lower)
Any other predominant color _____

4. **CLARITY** — Examine diamond carefully without loupe.
   1. Eye clean SI$_2$ or better _____
   2. Small but visible flaws. I$_1$ _____
   3. Easy to see from about a foot away but diamond still shines. I$_2$ _____
   4. Terrible flaws visible from a distance (looks like a hammer smashed it.) I$_3$ _____

If the diamond is definitely "eye clean," examine diamond in a loupe carefully (steady one hand against the other — focus and study diamond at *all* angles.) Take your time!

   1. Flaws are obvious, significant and/or numerous. SI$_2$ _____
   2. Flaws are easily visible but very moderate in size and number. SI$_1$ _____
   3. On immediate inspection, diamond appears clear but on close inspection, very small flaws appear. VS$_1$-VS$_2$ _____
   4. Diamond is 100 percent clean to the loupe. Possible VVS-VS$_1$ _____

Look up price charts on page _____. (If exact grade is questionable, average the high and low values). Deduct 5-20 percent for poor cut depending on how poor. Deduct 10 percent for off sizes.
LIST VALUE _____
SELLER'S ASKING PRICE _____

5. **COMMON SENSE**
   1. Don't be "pushed" into buying.
   2. Check other dealers and compare.
   3. Consider the cost of credit against a cash discount.

GOOD LUCK AND HAVE FUN!!!

SECTION 2

A History of Diamonds and Their Investment Value

CHAPTER 9

Diamonds: Where Have They Come From, Where Are They Headed?

The history, mystery, intrigue and fascination of diamonds goes back at least 2500 years and seems to be destined to titillate our imagination to the end of time. It may seem unfathomable that these small, shiny rocks have started wars in their history and continue to play a major symbolic role in millions of people's lives, but it's true.

The Bible says that when the Israelites wandered the desert for 40 years, God commanded them to create a breast plate as part of the High Priests' holy garment. In that breast plate, twelve precious stones were set. One of them was the "yahalom," presumed to be a large diamond.

In Zachariah, Chapter 7, Verse 12, the prophet tells us "they made their hearts as an adamant stone." This was probably referring to a diamond, a stone harder than any other. In Greek literature "Adamas," the root word of diamond, is associated with invincibility.

For many centuries diamonds came only from India. The ancients attributed great mystical powers to diamonds. They entered into the legends of Alexander the Great, Synbad the Sailor, and Marco Polo, among others. The great world trader, Tavernier, traded diamonds in the 1600's and sold Louis XIV many magnificent stones.

At first only kings were able to acquire these precious stones. They symbolized power, invincibility and courage. They were seen as powerful good luck charms. Ironically, it seems that women were prohibited from wearing diamonds, now "a girl's best friend," until the 15th Century. In the middle ages, astrologers attributed magical and protective powers to diamonds.

The stories that are attributed to famous and outstanding diamonds can fill volumes. Of the famous Koh-i-noor diamond, or "mountain of light," it is said that "He who possesses this diamond will possess the world, but he will also experience the worst misfortunes. Only a god or a woman can wear it with impunity." This smacks of today's general approach that the female species is entitled to be the wearer of the diamonds in the house, and maybe the pants as well.

The Koh-i-noor diamond influenced history for years. It is currently one of the British crown jewels and is traditionally worn only by female royalty.

The Orlov, the Hope Diamond, and the Regeant Diamond all have fascinating histories. Unfortunately, they are too long for our discussion here but well worth your research and study.

Making Good Under Pressure

Before discussing the development of today's diamond market, we will briefly explain the geologic developments of the diamonds themselves. Diamonds are one of the few substances that have reached the surface of the earth from its inner depths. Diamonds are essentially carbon or graphite that developed at depths of about 120 miles, in intense heat of 3600 degrees Fahrenheit and under intense pressure. Anything short of this intense heat and pressure yields ordinary carbon.

Diamonds by definition are pieces of carbon that have made good under pressure. As plentiful as diamonds seem to be, it still takes sifting through an average of one ton of blueground to produce one-half carat or one-tenth of a gram of diamond.

Modern science has had the technology for many years to synthesize diamonds and has successfully done so.

These are real diamonds. However, as expensive as these diamonds are, it is still much less costly to search for the natural ones than to create them artificially.

Diamonds reach the earth's surface through volcanic action in a volcanic ore called Kimberlite or Blueground. Many diamonds are mined out of these volcanic passageways or "pipes." A high percentage are found in old riverbeds that carried the diamonds as the earth eroded over the years. These diamond finds are called alluvial diamonds.

Of the diamonds mined, only twenty percent are gem quality. Even these show flaws that developed in their formation, similar to the air bubbles in ice cubes. A very, very small percentage are flawless or VVS and still a much smaller percentage will be relatively "clean" and have a fine color.

The Rise of a Monopoly

In the last 100 years, diamond history has changed drastically. India and then later Brazil were the prime sources of diamonds until 1866 when large concentrations of diamonds were discovered in South Africa. Diamond merchants were concerned that if diamonds were totally uncontrolled in open markets, the price of diamonds and interest in them would drop significantly.

This was prevented by a unique monopoly that started in 1888 when the DeBeers Consolidated Mines Limited was formed. It took years for DeBeers to gain control of the majority of the world diamond market. This was begun by Cecil Rhodes, and ultimately completed by Sir Ernest Oppenheimer in the 1930's.

Oppenheimer established the policy of trying to buy all available rough diamonds on the market and stockpiling them in order to control the market. He also initiated the syndicate's policy of allocating diamonds in quantities that maintain the prices in the world diamond market. This enabled diamonds to survive the depression of the 1930's. DeBeers stored diamonds in those years and they maintained their value.

DeBeers' Central Selling Organization (CSO) sells gem-quality rough diamonds to a mere 250 to 350 customers who disseminate them to diamond centers of the world. These customers, who pay a high price for the opportunity to buy from the CSO, are invited ten times a year to purchase "boxes" at the "sights" of rough diamonds in London. Each one of these customers has basically one choice: to take what DeBeers offers them or reject the box.

If the customer rejects the box, they jeopardize their future invitations back to the "sights," the ironic title given to this privilege of purchase.

DeBeers limits sales to a volume that keeps the market healthy and steadily, albeit slowly, rising, ensuring everyone's sound investment. DeBeers also promotes new marketing all over the world. The diamond engagement ring has become popular and traditional in every part of the world thanks to DeBeers advertising and marketing. This has kept the demand for diamonds strong through all kinds of world economic climates.

The Diamond "Boom" Bust

Recent diamond history has had its ups and downs. Diamond prices had been underpriced in the early and mid-1970's. The market adjusted in an upward trend significantly by 1978 and certain better grades of diamonds actually tripled their value.

For example, a one carat perfect diamond (D color flawless clarity) went from approximately $5,000 per carat to $15,000 per carat from 1970 to 1977. Gold paralleled that rise in the same period by going from $30 per ounce to nearly $300 per ounce.

In 1979 the diamond market went berserk. Everyone clamored to "invest in diamonds." This pushed the market past reasonable heights. As people watched the market rise, interest gained. This only served to spur the market on and strengthen the rise. Unfortunately, DeBeers accommodated this rising market and increased its sales.

During that period a D flawless diamond reached a height of $65,000 per carat in 1980. This market was likened to an overinflated balloon. When it finally popped in 1981, the market immediately dropped drastically. Doomsayers actually predicted that DeBeers would lose total control of the market by 1983. Numerous cutters, dealers and brokers went bankrupt. The entire diamond market looked bleak.

This unprecedented phenomenon was a real challenge to the DeBeers system. To most people's surprise, DeBeers was able to buy polished diamonds in the marketplace, stockpile them, and slowly, over a period of the next five years, stabilize the market. Although prices dropped drastically, they did not "bottom out" as many people think they did. Prices did return to the levels that made sense prior to the unnatural rise in prices. The D flawless fell to a $10,000-$12,000 level but never much below that.

The Recovery

In April 1986, DeBeers took a very bold step. They announced for the first time in five years a planned rise in the price of diamonds. At the May, 1986, sight in London, DeBeers raised prices an average of 7½ percent. The rise actually varied from approximately 3 percent in the inexpensive and smaller goods and up to 15 percent for many of the larger, finer rough material.

The reaction of the market has been extremely positive. Demand has increased. In many parts of the world, a boom is in progress. It seems evident that DeBeers has had the strength to ride out the storm and that DeBeers' strategy has returned the world diamond market to business as usual.

Many people have tried to compare monopolies such as OPEC to DeBeers, but obviously DeBeers has succeeded where OPEC and others have failed. While the OPEC cartel has hurt the world economy, DeBeers has served to protect the value of everyone's diamonds. As we go to press on this book, prices are rising and I've begun to get calls from pure investors, which has not occurred for some time.

What the future has in store for the diamond market, nobody knows. My hunch is that the only direction for diamonds to go is up. The fact that DeBeers has succeeded thus far will only help to maintain world confidence in diamonds. A recent article titled "DeBeers is Forever," a take-off on the "Diamonds are Forever" campaign DeBeers initiated, neatly sums up the current attitude.

The bottom line is that you can buy your diamonds with the confidence that they will retain value, and that they will be items of beauty for you to hand down from one generation to the next.

CHAPTER 10

Diamond Investment and Selling Your Diamond

Is a diamond a good investment? The answer to that question may depend on your definition of a "good investment." All I can impart to you is my personal opinion.

First of all, a wise old man once told me, "Anytime you give a lady a diamond to wear, it cannot be considered an investment." You'll never get it back to sell it! I guess if she's the right lady then she would be considered the investment.

To illustrate what diamonds can do over the long haul, I'll relate an interesting experience. About 3 years ago, a lovely elderly lady brought me a 3 carat diamond to appraise. I gave it a wholesale value of about $15,000 and offered her $12,000 cash if she wanted to sell.

She was·pleasantly surprised. It seems that approximately 25 years ago she had the choice of purchasing this diamond or a new car for $500 and she opted for the diamond. Calculating on the basis of current prices, I realized that a car today would run in the vicinity of $9000 to $15,000 and that this lady's diamond literally kept up with inflation.

The beautiful part of the story is that she wore and enjoyed this diamond, and it complimented her beauty for 25 years while retaining real value. That probably would not have been true for a car. One could say she made a good investment.

One point is certain: buying a diamond at 100 percent to 300 percent higher than its true market value will make it improbable to achieve the hedge or investment value we've discussed.

Whether or not a diamond is a good investment for you is directly related to the obstacles in selling that stone. A lady once asked me, "Why can you sell a diamond so easily and I can't?" I told her, "Invest $500,000 in an inventory, open up a store, work your tail off for a few years, and you'll be an 'instant' success."

Unfortunately, there is no real clearing house or trading market for diamonds. Because of the subtleties in determining what a diamond is and what it's worth, there probably never will be.

I feel diamonds are fun to wear and enjoy. If you buy the diamond at the right price and later want to trade up to a bigger one, you'll always find a dealer that will give you a good market value on the stone in partial trade for a bigger or better diamond. If you have to cash out of a diamond, you shouldn't have to take much of a loss if it was purchased at a good price. If you have held it over a period of time, you will probably profit nicely. Keep in mind, though, the dealer needs the incentive to buy from a private party rather than their usual cutter or broker and that usually means a significant price reduction under market.

Selling diamonds to other private parties is not easy, but will usually net you much more money and profit, especially if you find someone who would otherwise buy retail.

A young man came into my store a few years ago with his fiancee. They bought a ring and unfortunately broke their engagement shortly afterward. He decided to sell it privately and came in the following week to ask a surprising question.

"Could you sell me a couple more of those diamonds?" It seems he made a nice profit selling his engagement ring and thought he could repeat the trick and make more.

I'm pleased to tell you that he came in a year later with the fiancee he did marry. They brought their son in a year after that and we enjoyed the happy ending.

A good retail appraisal from a reputable jeweler will help you substantiate the grade and value to your customer. To find that customer, you may want to spread the word at work or among your friends that you have a diamond for sale. The information gleaned from this guide will of course give you an air of professionalism.

You may want to advertise in the newspaper classified section. But be careful! There are all kinds of "crazies" out there, and your safety and security of course is primary. Never show the diamond at home or even give your home address. I suggest you show the diamond only at a bank vault, and make it clear that you keep it there! Don't take any risks!! It's not worth it!

Many people will give stores or dealers their diamonds on consignment. If you give the dealer an incentive to sell your stone by giving the dealer a real price break, he may sell your diamond. If you don't, he'll probably sell his own. You may be disappointed to watch your diamond sit for a prolonged period of time in his showcase, offering free window dressing for the jeweler but no results for you.

The world of diamonds is fascinating, fun, and can be profitable. Buy them well, enjoy them and you'll find that their dividends can be genuinely rewarding.

SECTION 3

Gold Settings and Colored Stones:
There Are More Facets to Jewelry
Than The Ones On A Diamond

The major portion of this book has dealt with the subject of how to buy diamonds. I chose this specific gem topic for two reasons: the first was interest and experience. The second was that diamonds probably encompass the most dollars in lump sums spent in the jewelry area.

In order to round out this guide, I would like to offer you some pointers and tricks of the trade that may help you in your general jewelry buying. I will concentrate on how to evaluate gold jewelry and the most popular precious stone group, which includes emeralds, rubies, sapphires and pearls.

This additional information is by no means meant to be an exhaustive discussion, but I hope it will help you to not make some of the mistakes that I have made and that took years of experience to correct.

CHAPTER 11

All That Glitters Is Not Pure Gold

When buying gold jewelry, one is buying first and foremost art and ornamentation, and lastly precious metal. Beauty is in the eye of the beholder and I therefore believe that the first rule in jewelry buying is to buy what you like and what you'll wear — not just what is the least expensive and what may very well end up put away in some drawer or safe deposit box. On the other hand, when buying gold jewelry, you must know how to compare and find a good value for your money.

Carrots, Carats, and Karats

The first lesson in gold buying is to know the difference between carrot, karat, and carat. The first of the three, carrot, is the bright orange spear shaped vegetable that grows in the ground. It is tasty, sold by the pound, and will help improve your eyesight so you can enjoy seeing the other two varieties.

Mixtures of Gold

Carat, as we already learned while talking about diamonds, is a gem weight equal to 1/5 of a gram. Gem stones are weighed by the carat.

Karat (abbreviated kt.) is an important term when buying gold. It indicates the percentage of gold in any metal consisting of a gold and alloy mixture. Pure, refined 100 percent gold is 24 karat gold. Gold in its natural state can vary from near 24 karat all the way to only 50 percent gold (12 kt).

I recently purchased four ounces of natural Alaskan

placer nuggets that assayed at only 60 percent gold or slightly better than 14 karat. This is because the nuggets naturally are mixed with rock and soil and other substances. Coincidentally, I've recently negotiated on purchasing gold dust from the Ivory Coast that assayed at 95 percent pure, or at about 23 karat. To get gold to its 99.9 percent pure form, you must refine it.

Pure gold is rarely used in this country for jewelry making. In other parts of the world such as Asia, especially where the people not only wear gold for ornamentation but also to keep their "bank accounts" close and around their necks, 20-24 karat gold is the norm. These people find our 14 karat gold variety "cheap".

In some countries, such as England, the norm has been as low as 9 karat or about 37 percent gold and 63 percent alloy. Our society views this combination as being "cheap".

The accepted norm in America is primarily 14 karat, or 58.5 percent gold and 41.5 percent other metal alloys. Eighteen karat or 75 percent gold is often used and considered "classier". Ten karat or 41.5 percent gold is often used in class rings and other emblematic jewelry and is not considered as prestigious.

The bottom line when buying jewelry is to understand how much gold is in that item and know what it's worth to make sure you are getting your value for your money. Most American jewelry is stamped 10 kt., 14 kt., or 18 kt. European jewelry, on the other hand, is stamped based on the percentage of gold content. For example, 14 kt. is stamped 585 for 58.5 percent and 18 kt. gold is stamped 750 for 75 percent gold.

Pure gold is a bright yellow-gold color. Gold can be alloyed with other metals to strengthen it and give it different colors. If one alloys the gold with pure copper, it will give the gold a reddish or rose color. Mixing white metals, such as nickel and silver, with gold results in a white color, hence white gold. Yellow gold can vary in its color from bright gold-yellow to a much softer hue depending on the mixture of the alloying metals.

Dollar Values in Gold Jewelry

What is gold jewelry worth? There are a number of factors that establish cost and value. The way to figure out the value of gold jewelry begins with the value of the gold content. A gold salesperson should be able to weigh the item for you in either grams or pennyweight (abbreviated DWT). There are 31.1 grams per ounce and 20 DWT per ounce. If a ring, for example, weighs ½ ounce, it will weight 10 DWT or will weigh 15.55 grams.

To find out the value of the gold content, first multiply the current price per ounce of pure gold times the karat percentage. You will find the current New York and/or London gold price fix in almost every daily newspaper.

If the current value of gold is $420.00 an ounce, multiply 58.5 percent times $420.00 to find out what one ounce of 14 karat gold is worth. Your answer will be $245.70 for one full ounce of 14 karat gold. Divide this figure either by 31.1 for the gram value ($7.90 per gram), or divide by 20 for the DWT value ($12.29 per DWT). Now that you have the value per gram or DWT, multiply the weight of the ring (1/2 ounce or 15.55 gram or 10 DWT) and you have the gold content value in that ring ($122.85) (see illustration #19).

Design and Value

This is only the beginning of your valuation. To know the value of the piece of jewely you must add labor, creativity, and both the wholesale and the retail mark ups. All these factors add up to the true value of the ring. Generally speaking, the less labor and creativity involved in making the jewelry, the less the jewelry should sell for. The more labor intensive, the more it's worth and the more you would have to pay.

Standard patterns in gold chains are the least expensive items in the jewelry line. This is because they are usually manufactured completely with machines where the gold is fed in at one end and the chain emerges from the other with a minimal amount of labor.

$$\begin{array}{r} \$420.00 \\ \times\ 58.5\,\% \\ \hline \end{array}$$

$$1\,oz.\ 14\,kt\ gold = \$245.70$$

$$\begin{array}{r} \$245.70/oz. \\ \div\ 31.10\ grams/oz. \\ \hline \$7.90/gram \end{array} \quad OR \quad \begin{array}{r} \$245.70/oz. \\ \div\ 20.00\ DWT/oz. \\ \hline \$12.29\ /DWT \end{array}$$

$$\begin{array}{r} \$7.90/gram \\ \times\ 15.55\ grams \\ \hline \$122.85 \end{array} \qquad \begin{array}{r} \$12.29/DWT \\ \times\ 10\ DWT \\ \hline \$122.85 \end{array}$$

gold content value
of ring

Illustration 19: Gold value computation

In this case, if you add the gold value, the labor, and reasonable mark ups, you should be able to buy the chain at about three times the gold value. This includes a fairly healthy retail mark up. Chain can sell for as much as eight times the gold value. Intelligent shopping should help you find dealers with reasonable mark ups.

On the other extreme, a custom designed piece of jewelry by a high-priced designer may run as much as twelve times or fifteen times the gold value. In addition, one would have to add for extra labor such as stone setting. If a piece is extremely light, it may run even higher because the same labor is spread over less gold.

The best value, I have found, can come from local goldsmiths. You can get finer customized design at a price that only reflects one mark up. At my store, Jay Feder Jewelers in Denver, we offer this option, and a high percentage of our customers take advantage of it both for beauty and value (see illustration #20).

Once again, comparison shopping will insure the best deal. Don't be fooled by sales. After all, if you mark an item up ten times that of wholesale, fifty percent off is still an exorbitant price.

Last Christmas I monitored a local department store's handling of a standard chain for which I was paying $75.00. Their retail price was $500. On sale it was reduced to $249. Knowing gold values and using the computation above, you don't need advanced math to know that's no "deal."

Don't be afraid to compare prices to get a feel for the market and don't be ashamed to have a salesman weigh the piece in front of you. Consumers in Europe and Asia have been buying based on weight for years and years and this is the way the store bought its chain and jewelry.

With a little extra effort and thought your gold "prospecting" can yield the real thing that glitters. A "blind" purchase may net you only fool's gold.

Illustration 20: **"Duet"** His & Hers Wedding Set,
designed by Douglas Geivett,
a **De Beers** award-winner.

CHAPTER 12

From C to Shining C
Colored Stones

As a preface to our mini-course on buying emeralds, rubies, sapphires, and pearls, I would like to emphasize the differences in evaluating these stones and evaluating diamonds. The majority of this book has been dedicated to the four Cs that go into the evaluation of diamonds and the importance of balancing these four Cs. In fact, for that reason we added the last two Cs: common sense and cost. At the risk of making you C-sick, we're up to the seventh C: the color in colored stones.

The most difficult lesson I've had in the study of colored stones is my temptation to try to compare them exactly with diamonds and my ultimate realization that they are totally different.

Although we are comparing gems and they all have color, cut, clarity, and carat weight, the relative importance of the cut, the carat weight, and the clarity is much less. All those factors are dwarfed by the importance of color.

As we'll explain further, cut does make a difference but only if it's extremely poor. Poor clarity does make a difference, but we don't study colored stones with loupes to the extent that we do with a diamond. As long as the stone is basically eye-clean, inclusions are not that important in colored stones.

And last but not least, although carat does make a difference, we don't split hairs as far as exact weights or "magic numbers" as we do in diamonds. I hope we will both C I to I on this very important matter.

Color Evaluation

In each type of precious stone, as you will see, there are preferred colors and secondary colors. Taking into account our usual rule of thumb that you must look for colors you enjoy and find appealing, let me offer a grading system used by experienced colored stone dealers.

Using a scale of one to one hundred, imagine that one is colorless and one hundred is black or full intensity of the particular color in question. In that system, ideal color would fall between sixty-five and seventy-five degrees of intensity on the 1-100 scale. The color at 50 degrees of intensity would be too light to be ideal. More than seventy-five degrees of intensity would begin to lose the beautiful transparency of a fine gem. Despite what I have just said, remember that the bottom line still is "Beauty is in the eye of the beholder."

CHAPTER 13

Emeralds

An emerald is as valued and as precious as a diamond. It is probably more difficult to find gem quality emeralds than any of the other stones we are discussing.

Emeralds were first mined commercially by Cleopatra's workers in Egypt. Most mining today is concentrated in Columbia, South America, and in what is now Zambia in Africa. Emeralds are known by the mine they come from and the most famous among them is the Muzo mine in Columbia.

As with rubies and sapphires, emeralds are given trade names based on either where they come from or by the color that is common to the country used in the name. Columbian emeralds are considered the finest emeralds in the world. A fine Columbian emerald is a deep green color. Its secondary color or its undertones would be a yellowish color. Zambian or African emeralds can also have a deep, green color, but generally have more of a blue secondary color or undertone.

It is important to remember that emeralds have been greatly imitated and synthesized. There are three main companies that synthesize or create man-made emeralds. These are often referred to by the company names which are Chatham, Linde, and Gilson emeralds. It is important to purchase emeralds from sources that can tell the difference and know that their emeralds are genuine and not man-made.

Cut

Emeralds will be cut far more often in the emerald cut shape than in other shapes, but of course they are available in almost any shape as well. Emerald is a rather fragile stone. Although it is very hard, because of the usual type of inclusions in the stone it is quite easily broken and fractured. This, in fact, is why the emerald cut developed without corners, because inevitably the corners on emeralds would break off. Even the best stone setters will often refuse to set emeralds and almost never take any responsibility because of their fragility.

I know that when I am setting numerous small emeralds, I will always match an extra few because I'm almost assured of some breakage. I personally do not suggest that people buy emeralds for rings that they will wear all the time.

Again, although the cut is not that important, stones that are totally lopsided, totally non-symmetrical, are of lesser value. Stones whose "belly," or bottom of the stone, is much too deep, gives the stone a much lighter impression than its true weight and should be avoided.

Clarity

It is next to impossible to find an emerald that is completely clean or flawless. Almost every emerald has what we refer to as a garden, which means a web of inclusions and flaws. One should try to avoid emerald flaws that are extremely noticeable to the naked eye, but don't expect it to be completely eye-clean either.

Color

The tone and the hue of the emerald is the most important factor. The hue should be a medium dark green color and the tone should be a medium dark green color as well. As mentioned earlier, the finest Columbian emeralds have a slight bit of yellow undertone. Stones that are much too dark or stones that are much too light drop drastically in value.

Value

The value of emeralds has increased tremendously in the last few years. Fine emeralds are getting more and more difficult to find. This important fact serves only to emphasize that, when buying an emerald, one shops and compares. The deals are there to be found, but you must work at it because it won't happen by itself.

When buying emeralds, again, color is everything. Try to make sure that the color has the tone that you like, that the stone is not milky but rather has good brilliance and transparency. Also, beware of internal fractures, stress points that may cause the stone to be much less durable and may ultimately leave you with more than one stone.

People who like emerald green color and want a more durable stone and find that the emeralds are too expensive may want to buy stones such as tsavorite garnet, peridot, or green tourmaline as semi-precious substitutes.

CHAPTER 14
Rubies

Rubies and sapphires both belong to the family of stones called corundum. All pieces of red corundum are rubies. All others, even pinks, are sapphires.

The main source of fine rubies is Burma. They are also found in Ceylon and Thailand. Corundum is the hardest mineral after diamond. Although it is only 1/140 as hard, it is still seven times as hard as topaz, which is the next level on the hardness scale.

As we explained with emeralds, the most important factor in rubies is color. There are different trade names for the different colors. Burma rubies are generally light red toward pink, but the deep, dark "pigeon-blood" color is the best. Ceylon rubies are very light pink or red with kind of purplish undertones. Generally speaking, the redder the stone, the finer the stone; the more purple, the more violet the stone, the less expensive, the less valuable.

My personal preference in rubies, although I like them as red as possible, are rubies that have some lighter highlights. This way, when you look at them, they shine back at you. I personally do not prefer rubies that are so deep and dark that you don't get a feeling of light going through them. This, however, is up to your personal aesthetic judgment.

As we explained earlier with emeralds, synthetic rubies are not uncommon. Generally, the finer looking the stone, the greater the chance of having a synthetic rather than an authentic stone. Always make sure you are purchasing the stone from a reputable source that will help ensure its authenticity.

Clarity

Again, ideally one would like to buy a clean stone, that is, clean to the naked eye. But this is very rare. As soon as inclusions become very obvious to the naked eye, values begin to drop. Make sure the stone is not cloudy and not milky, but rather very intense, transparent with good color sparkling to the eye.

Cut

The best and most common cut for rubies is an oval shape, although rubies come in all shapes. Try to make sure that the ruby shows off its weight for its size and does not have a "belly" that is too deep. On the other hand, a ruby that is too thin or shallow may appear too transparent and lose its color intensity.

Carat Weight

The weight of the ruby is not as crucial as in diamonds until you get to much larger rubies, from approximately two carats and up. At that point, they actually become a lot more rare than diamonds would be in those sizes and the prices and values increase significantly. Very small rubies, on the other hand, should be very inexpensive.

Rubies that are not very transparent are often cut into star rubies. A star ruby is one that has been made into a "cabochon," where what would usually be the bottom of the ruby becomes the top of the ruby. It is rounded as opposed to faceted. A nice star ruby will produce the reflection of a star in the center of the stone. Star rubies should be much less expensive than faceted stones. When they get into a muddy, brownish hue they become very inexpensive.

No matter what type of ruby you buy, your chief consideration again should be color and the overall personality of the stone. Make sure its personality gets along with your personality.

CHAPTER 15
Sapphires

As we mentioned in the last chapter, sapphire belongs to the corundum family. Sapphires come in all colors. Generally, when one mentions a sapphire without ascribing color, one refers to a blue sapphire. All other sapphires must be mentioned with their color, such as a yellow sapphire, black star sapphire, etc.

Although, as we mentioned, rubies are rarely found in large sizes, sapphires are often found in very large sizes. The most important sources of fine sapphires are Burma, Ceylon, Thailand, Australia and increasingly high numbers of sapphires are coming from our own Montana in the U.S. of A.

As with rubies and emeralds, sapphires have their own trade names that refer to where they were mined. The finest and most expensive sapphires are Kashmir sapphires. These sapphires have a particularly velvety violet blue color, sometimes referred to as a cornflower blue. They are quite rare.

Burma sapphires are very fine as well. They have a rich royal blue color, sometimes with a little bit of violet. Ceylon sapphires are generally a lighter blue color. They are usually quite brilliant and frequently they have a zoning problem which means that their coloring is uneven throughout the stone. Australian sapphires are very, very dark, quite often having a green hue to them.

Our own Montana sapphires, or Yogo sapphires, are generally a very light color. In the U.S., larger stones are extremely unusual and our mines produce primarily half carat stones and under. There has recently been a big push to market these sapphires, but I have not found them to be that popular.

Color

When buying a sapphire, as with a ruby and an emerald, color is fundamental. Different people have different preferences in terms of the depth and the intensity of color. Some people like them extremely dark, other people like them to have more personality and more light play.

Most sapphires on the market have green or gray undertones. The main thing is to try to get them as blue as possible, as opposed to gray and green. Other colored sapphires, such as yellow sapphires, green, orange, etc., are much less expensive than the blue sapphire. The one exception is the pinkish-orange or podparasha, which is very rare and valuable. Remember, if it's a piece of corundum that is pink or rose colored, it is referred to as a sapphire, not a ruby.

Cut

As in rubies, the primary shape is oval although they can be cut in every different shape. Sapphires that are more opaque are often cut into star sapphires, just as we have explained with star rubies. Some star sapphires can get quite expensive, depending on their quality. On the other hand, black star sapphires are very inexpensive.

When buying sapphires, as with any other stone, shop and compare. Try to find the color you like with a maximum amount of transparency and intensity.

Remember, shop and compare. You will be amazed at the differences in price in a market for similar quality stones.

CHAPTER 16
Pearls

I offer you a bit of wisdom I've gathered about pearls or, shall we say, some "Pearls of Wisdom."

Let's begin by explaining the difference between cultured and natural pearls. Both are produced by mollusks, usually oyster.

When an irritant becomes lodged between the oyster's inner skin and the shell, the oyster's protective secretion forms a pearl. Natural pearls form when sand or another natural irritant gets into the oyster's shell. Cultured pearls form when an irritant is deliberately inserted. Today, at least 90 percent of the pearls on the market are cultured. An entire strand of natural pearls would be very expensive.

I recently had the opportunity to sell a large natural pearl. First of all, finding it was next to impossible. Once we finally found sources for these pearls, the price differentials were incredible. We ultimately sold the pearl wholesale for approximately $10,000 for one 16-millimeter pear-shaped pearl. And this pearl sold for one-third the price of similar pearls in Paris and London where they were even harder to find.

There are actually more factors in judging pearls than there are in judging any other colored stone or diamond. Those factors are size, hue, luster, roundness, finish, and the reliability of the dealer.

Size
Pearls are graded by the millimeter diameter. Generally

speaking, pearls up to 4 to 4½ millimeters in diameter are rarely expensive. Five to 7½ millimeters get quite a bit higher. When you get over 7½, into the 8 millimeter category and over, the availability decreases and the price increases tremendously.

Basically, even with cultured pearls, most oysters or mollusks will be growing the smaller pearls. When you get over an 8 millimeter pearl, you are talking about an oyster that had great longevity. I often tell my customers that on a strand of 8½ to 9 millimeter pearls, each pearl would come from an oyster that lived the equivalent of 120 years. How many 120 year olds do you know? Their rarity, of course, adds to value and cost.

Pearls are always measured in increments of ½ millimeters. For instance, you would buy a strand of pearls that range from 5 to 5½ millimeters, 5½ to 6, 6 to 6½, 6½ to 7, 7 to 7½, 7½ to 8, etc. When comparing pearls, keep in mind that the sizes make a big difference in the price and always compare two like sizes when price shopping.

Hue

Once you determine the size of the pearl you like or can afford, the next most important factor is the color of the pearl. There are actually, according to some, 80 different hues in the color of pearls. It's amazing when you really sit and compare colors. Even colors that seem similar will vary in secondary hues and will vary in degree of translucency. Some of these color factors are next to impossible to explain in words — they have to be seen.

Popular colors range from the pink rosé, which is the most popular, a white color with a rosé tinge ranging into the white ranges all the way into the cream colors. Fine rosé are considered the most expensive, the creamier pearls are much less expensive.

It is important to take into consideration when buying pearls what color you prefer and what color looks good against your particular skin tone. One important trick in judging color is not to judge the color against a black cloth, which is the usual way for showing pearls, but rather judge color of the pearls against a white background.

Insist on a white background. You will be amazed at the color differential that shows up with a white background as opposed to black velvet. Make sure that in the strand of pearls the colors are well matched. Watch out for dull or dingy colors which are much less valuable.

Luster

Luster is the high intensity shine that a good pearl should have. The luster is one of the factors that gives the pearl its unique beauty. Aside from that, the luster also indicates how thick the nacre or outer layer skin of the pearl is. The finer the luster, the thicker the outer layer it has. This will enable the pearl to last longer and retain its beauty. Try to find pearls that have a very high luster.

Roundness

Make sure that in the strand of pearls each pearl is round, not off-round. Slightly off-round to off-round pearls are called semi baroque to baroque pearls and generally are much less valuable. They are often sold in strands which are not matched. Some will be round and some will be slightly off-round. Try to make sure all the pearls in the strand are perfectly round, or plan on paying a lot less. The more off shape, the less expensive they should be.

Finish

Try to avoid pearls that have scratches, dents, cracks, or uneven surfaces. White splotches or other blemishes detract from the pearl's beauty. Pearls that have real cracks in them are almost worthless.

Today's Market

You will find that variations from perfection in all these different areas will make a big difference in the pearls' cost and a big difference in their value. As in all gem stones, shop, compare, examine, and don't be afraid to ask questions.

The price of pearls has risen tremendously in the last few years. This is because pearls mainly come from the Orient and the value of the yen has increased relative to the dollar. Therefore, if you purchased pearls 10 and 15 years ago, don't expect to purchase pearls for any similar price today.

Today we are in the midst of the most extreme American currency drop in years. Some dealers may have had old inventory they bought for less than new inventory that they are currently buying. Therefore you can see that the age of the inventory is another factor that may cause a tremendous differential in prices in the market.

Look for Reliability, Not Brand Names

If you buy pearls from a reputable store or dealer, you can rest assured that they are cultured pearls. Quite often people go with brand names such a Mikimoto. This is named after the K. Mikimoto who has long been believed to be the originator of cultured pearls. Very simply, all cultured pearls are created by essentially the same process. Therefore, it's difficult to understand that Mikimoto pearls are finer than anybody else's pearls. Don't pay a premium because somebody's given them a name.

As we mentioned earlier, there are big differences in value between natural pearls and cultured pearls. The only way to really tell the difference between the two today is via x-rays. X-rays show whether the irritant was natural or a man-made bead.

If one is buying natural pearls, one should have them checked out by the GIA, because it is impossible otherwise to tell whether they are really natural or simply the usual cultured pearl. Buying from a very reliable source should also suffice.

Beads

Of course everyone knows that there are huge amounts of imitation pearls on the market. These are really not pearls but rather man-made beads. One way to tell the difference between the two is to take the pearl and rub it lightly against your front tooth. If it is a bead rather than a pearl, it will be extremely smooth. If it is a pearl, it will have a slight roughness or grit to it against your tooth because a real pearl is just a series of calcium deposits, very thin layers. This will be evident on that kind of contact. You need your own teeth for this test. False teeth don't have the sensitivity.

On Stringing Pearls

When buying pearls, make sure all the pearls are well matched, well blended, and that everything seems to fit right in the strand. Make sure that all the pearls are drilled through the center and that when you hold the strand out they're all lined up evenly. If the pearls were not drilled properly, they will not look even on the strand and they will vary in position relative to each other.

Make sure the holes are not drilled too large. This will make the pearls loose on the string and again give an uneven look. Pearls are imported in groups or hanks. An unstrung strand of pearls is generally 16 inches long. When strung with the knots this would be somewhere around 18 or 19 inches long. Smaller pearls will string longer because there will be more knots on the strand and, of course, more knots will add more length. Large pearls will have fewer knots because in 16 inches you'll have fewer pearls to have knots in between.

Some companies string 18 inch strands and don't give you the few extra pearls that would result from stringing the 16 inch strand. There is nothing wrong if that is the length you like. But keep in mind, fewer pearls means less value and, when comparing, that can make a difference.

Generally speaking, one strand is referred to as a choker-length. One and a half strands or 24 inches (which can be strung anywhere from 24 to 28 inches, depending on the size of the pearls) is referred to as a matinee length. Two full strands, which would run from 32 to about 36 or 37 inches is referred to as an opera-length strand.

I often advise my customers to buy the longer strands. If they want to wear the strand shorter, they can always use a little device called a pearl shortener. This will shorten the length of the pearls and basically allow you to hide the pearls that you do not want showing behind your neck or under your collar. A pearl shortener will also allow you to take a single strand of pearls and double it so it looks like you're wearing a double strand.

A good salesperson can give you many suggestions on how to take a strand of pearls and wear it in many different styles. One long strand of fine pearls can become extremely versatile. If you buy a short one now with the idea of lengthening it later, you may have trouble finding a good match.

Graduated Strands

Finally, let me explain the difference between an even strand of the same size pearls and a strand of graduated pearls. Graduated pearls are not as popular as they used to be. The term means that the strand starts with a smaller pearl graduating to larger pearls in the center. Keep in mind that you will have many more small pearls than large pearls in a graduated strand. Therefore, the value should be weighted toward the smaller pearls rather than the larger pearls. Take note of the proportion of large pearls to that of small ones, by noting how quickly the sizes change as you review the length. The range of sizes should be noted from the millimeter size of the smallest to that of the largest. Using a rough count to establish proportions, try to base the value on the average size pearl.

Pearls are very exciting, very beautiful, and quite complicated. At the risk of being redundant, always compare, always shop, and do not be too shy to be assertive. The salespeople need you more than you need them.

CHAPTER 17

Parting Words

"It's easier with a comb." There I go, splitting hairs again! All kidding aside, I hope this book has aided you by opening up the beautiful world of diamonds and jewelry. I hope you've learned to be a more educated and aware consumer.

I know that I run the risk of sounding unfashionably patriotic. But I believe we are very fortunate to be living in a country where information such as what we've written can be published and offered to the public.

In my industry, our economic system has begun cutting out the layers of fat between the manufacturers and the consumer, offering to the consumer the opportunity to get more for their money than before. If this book aids the consumer in reaching that goal, it will all have been worthwhile.

Feel free to contact me and my crew for any additional information. We pledge to share our knowledge and expertise whenever and wherever possible. To reach us by phone call 1 (800) 262-0101 • Inside Colorado (303) 534-0251.

Last, but definitely not least, have fun, enjoy, and may your life "sparkle" like a diamond.

LIST OF ILLUSTRATIONS

DIAMOND BUYER'S CHECKLIST

1. CARAT WEIGHT _____
Off Size: Yes _____ No _____

2. CUT — Shape (Circle Correct One)
      Round   Brilliant   Marquise   Pear Shape
      Emerald Cut   Heart Shape   Radiant Cut
      Other _____
  Diamond is loose, not mounted:
      Yes _____ No _____
      Table: Small _____ Medium _____
            Large _____ Too Large _____
      Depth: Too Deep (Chunky) _____ Good _____
            Reasonable _____
            Shallow (Pancake) _____
      Girdle: Too Thin (Knife Edge) _____
            Thin _____ Medium _____
            Thick _____ Very Thick _____
      Brilliance: Magnificent _____ Nice _____
            Dull or Dark _____
            Something's Very Wrong _____
      Cutlet: Small _____ Medium _____
            Large _____ Is it an old cut? _____
      Fancy Shape: Bow Tie: Hardly Noticeable _____
            Noticeable _____ Very Prominent? _____

3. COLOR — Are you viewing the diamond in good natural light or a light box against a white background? (If not, stop right there!!)   Yes _____ No _____
If you have certified comparison grade stones: The

diamond comes closest to _____ comparison stone.
Without comparison grade stone: No discernible tint or color-colorless (D,E,F) _____
Very, very, slight tint upside down and looks real white right side up (G-H) _____
Slight tint upside down — still looks quite white right side up (I-J) _____
Definite light yellow (K,L,M or lower)
Any other predominant color _____

4. **CLARITY** — Examine diamond carefully without loupe.
   1. Eye clean SI_2 or better _____
   2. Small but visible flaws. I_1 _____
   3. Easy to see from about a foot away but diamond still shines. I_2 _____
   4. Terrible flaws visible from a distance (looks like a hammer smashed it.) I_3 _____

If the diamond is definitely "eye clean," examine diamond in a loupe carefully (steady one hand against the other — focus and study diamond at *all* angles.) Take your time!

   1. Flaws are obvious, significant and/or numerous. SI_2 _____
   2. Flaws are easily visible but very moderate in size and number. SI_1 _____
   3. On immediate inspection, diamond appears clear but on close inspection, very small flaws appear. VS_1-VS_2 _____
   4. Diamond is 100 percent clean to the loupe. Possible VVS-VS_1 _____

Look up price charts on page _____. (If exact grade is questionable, average the high and low values). Deduct 5-20 percent for poor cut depending on how poor. Deduct 10 percent for off sizes.
LIST VALUE _____
SELLER'S ASKING PRICE _____

5. **COMMON SENSE**
   1. Don't be "pushed" into buying.
   2. Check other dealers and compare.
   3. Consider the cost of credit against a cash discount.

ABOUT THE AUTHOR

Jay Feder and his wife, Celia, are the owners and operators of Jay Feder Jewelers.

Jay learned the ins and outs of the business quickly when, in 1977 he went on the road as a salesman for a major South African diamond cutter. As he covered a territory extending from Seattle to San Diego to Denver, he saw the myriad of hands a diamond passes through, with the mark-up that accompanies each one.

In 1979, Jay and Celia returned to Denver and bought a 40 year-old retail jewelry business. He transformed the store from the traditional low volume high mark up indirect sale of diamonds, to one with its own wholesale supply source. He found he was able to price from 50 to 150 percent below the competition and make up the difference with the high volume of sales to customers eager for a better deal.

As part of his service to his customers, Jay developed a 15 minute diamond lesson to help them in the comparison shopping. As more and more customers shopped around and came back convinced, they began to encourage Jay to turn the lesson into a book.

Jay has gained experience as a wholesale and retail diamond dealer whose close contact with every step of jewelry manufacture and distribution (along with his ready supply of jokes and puns), makes him the ideal person to help consumers get the best diamond for the best price.